KYRGYZ

VOCABULARY

FOR ENGLISH SPEAKERS

ENGLISH-KYRGYZ

The most useful words
To expand your lexicon and sharpen
your language skills

7000 words

Kyrgyz vocabulary for English speakers - 7000 words

By Andrey Taranov

T&P Books vocabularies are intended for helping you learn, memorize and review foreign words. The dictionary is divided into themes, covering all major spheres of everyday activities, business, science, culture, etc.

The process of learning words using T&P Books' theme-based dictionaries gives you the following advantages:

- Correctly grouped source information predetermines success at subsequent stages of word memorization
- Availability of words derived from the same root allowing memorization of word units (rather than separate words)
- Small units of words facilitate the process of establishing associative links needed for consolidation of vocabulary
- Level of language knowledge can be estimated by the number of learned words

T&P Books Publishing
www.tpbooks.com

ISBN: 978-1-78767-010-5

This book is also available in E-book formats.
Please visit www.tpbooks.com or the major online bookstores.

KYRGYZ VOCABULARY
for English speakers

T&P Books vocabularies are intended to help you learn, memorize, and review foreign words. The vocabulary contains over 7000 commonly used words arranged thematically.

- Vocabulary contains the most commonly used words
- Recommended as an addition to any language course
- Meets the needs of beginners and advanced learners of foreign languages
- Convenient for daily use, revision sessions, and self-testing activities
- Allows you to assess your vocabulary

Special features of the vocabulary

- Words are organized according to their meaning, not alphabetically
- Words are presented in three columns to facilitate the reviewing and self-testing processes
- Words in groups are divided into small blocks to facilitate the learning process
- The vocabulary offers a convenient and simple transcription of each foreign word

The vocabulary has 198 topics including:

Basic Concepts, Numbers, Colors, Months, Seasons, Units of Measurement, Clothing & Accessories, Food & Nutrition, Restaurant, Family Members, Relatives, Character, Feelings, Emotions, Diseases, City, Town, Sightseeing, Shopping, Money, House, Home, Office, Working in the Office, Import & Export, Marketing, Job Search, Sports, Education, Computer, Internet, Tools, Nature, Countries, Nationalities and more ...

T&P BOOKS' THEME-BASED DICTIONARIES

The Correct System for Memorizing Foreign Words

Acquiring vocabulary is one of the most important elements of learning a foreign language, because words allow us to express our thoughts, ask questions, and provide answers. An inadequate vocabulary can impede communication with a foreigner and make it difficult to understand a book or movie well.

The pace of activity in all spheres of modern life, including the learning of modern languages, has increased. Today, we need to memorize large amounts of information (grammar rules, foreign words, etc.) within a short period. However, this does not need to be difficult. All you need to do is to choose the right training materials, learn a few special techniques, and develop your individual training system.

Having a system is critical to the process of language learning. Many people fail to succeed in this regard; they cannot master a foreign language because they fail to follow a system comprised of selecting materials, organizing lessons, arranging new words to be learned, and so on. The lack of a system causes confusion and eventually, lowers self-confidence.

T&P Books' theme-based dictionaries can be included in the list of elements needed for creating an effective system for learning foreign words. These dictionaries were specially developed for learning purposes and are meant to help students effectively memorize words and expand their vocabulary.

Generally speaking, the process of learning words consists of three main elements:

- Reception (creation or acquisition) of a training material, such as a word list
- Work aimed at memorizing new words
- Work aimed at reviewing the learned words, such as self-testing

All three elements are equally important since they determine the quality of work and the final result. All three processes require certain skills and a well-thought-out approach.

New words are often encountered quite randomly when learning a foreign language and it may be difficult to include them all in a unified list. As a result, these words remain written on scraps of paper, in book margins, textbooks, and so on. In order to systematize such words, we have to create and continually update a "book of new words." A paper notebook, a netbook, or a tablet PC can be used for these purposes.

This "book of new words" will be your personal, unique list of words. However, it will only contain the words that you came across during the learning process. For example, you might have written down the words "Sunday," "Tuesday," and "Friday." However, there are additional words for days of the week, for example, "Saturday," that are missing, and your list of words would be incomplete. Using a theme dictionary, in addition to the "book of new words," is a reasonable solution to this problem.

The theme-based dictionary may serve as the basis for expanding your vocabulary.

It will be your big "book of new words" containing the most frequently used words of a foreign language already included. There are quite a few theme-based dictionaries available, and you should ensure that you make the right choice in order to get the maximum benefit from your purchase.

Therefore, we suggest using theme-based dictionaries from T&P Books Publishing as an aid to learning foreign words. Our books are specially developed for effective use in the sphere of vocabulary systematization, expansion and review.

Theme-based dictionaries are not a magical solution to learning new words. However, they can serve as your main database to aid foreign-language acquisition. Apart from theme dictionaries, you can have copybooks for writing down new words, flash cards, glossaries for various texts, as well as other resources; however, a good theme dictionary will always remain your primary collection of words.

T&P Books' theme-based dictionaries are specialty books that contain the most frequently used words in a language.

The main characteristic of such dictionaries is the division of words into themes. For example, the *City* theme contains the words "street," "crossroads," "square," "fountain," and so on. The *Talking* theme might contain words like "to talk," "to ask," "question," and "answer".

All the words in a theme are divided into smaller units, each comprising 3–5 words. Such an arrangement improves the perception of words and makes the learning process less tiresome. Each unit contains a selection of words with similar meanings or identical roots. This allows you to learn words in small groups and establish other associative links that have a positive effect on memorization.

The words on each page are placed in three columns: a word in your native language, its translation, and its transcription. Such positioning allows for the use of techniques for effective memorization. After closing the translation column, you can flip through and review foreign words, and vice versa. "This is an easy and convenient method of review – one that we recommend you do often."

Our theme-based dictionaries contain transcriptions for all the foreign words. Unfortunately, none of the existing transcriptions are able to convey the exact nuances of foreign pronunciation. That is why we recommend using the transcriptions only as a supplementary learning aid. Correct pronunciation can only be acquired with the help of sound. Therefore our collection includes audio theme-based dictionaries.

The process of learning words using T&P Books' theme-based dictionaries gives you the following advantages:

- You have correctly grouped source information, which predetermines your success at subsequent stages of word memorization
- Availability of words derived from the same root (lazy, lazily, lazybones), allowing you to memorize word units instead of separate words
- Small units of words facilitate the process of establishing associative links needed for consolidation of vocabulary
- You can estimate the number of learned words and hence your level of language knowledge
- The dictionary allows for the creation of an effective and high-quality revision process
- You can revise certain themes several times, modifying the revision methods and techniques
- Audio versions of the dictionaries help you to work out the pronunciation of words and develop your skills of auditory word perception

The T&P Books' theme-based dictionaries are offered in several variants differing in the number of words: 1.500, 3.000, 5.000, 7.000, and 9.000 words. There are also dictionaries containing 15,000 words for some language combinations. Your choice of dictionary will depend on your knowledge level and goals.

We sincerely believe that our dictionaries will become your trusty assistant in learning foreign languages and will allow you to easily acquire the necessary vocabulary.

TABLE OF CONTENTS

PRONUNCIATION GUIDE

T&P phonetic alphabet	Kyrgyz example	English example
[a]	манжа [mandʒa]	shorter than in ask
[e]	келечек [keletʃek]	elm, medal
[i]	жигит [dʒigit]	shorter than in feet
[ɪ]	кубаныч [kubanɪtʃ]	big, America
[o]	мактоо [maktoo]	pod, John
[u]	узундук [uzunduk]	book
[ʉ]	алюминий [alʉminij]	youth, usually
[y]	түнкү [tynky]	fuel, tuna
[b]	ашкабак [aʃkabak]	baby, book
[d]	адам [adam]	day, doctor
[dʒ]	жыгач [dʒɪgatʃ]	joke, general
[f]	флейта [flejta]	face, food
[g]	тегерек [tegerek]	game, gold
[j]	бөйрөк [bøjrøk]	yes, New York
[k]	карапа [karapa]	clock, kiss
[l]	алтын [altɪn]	lace, people
[m]	бешмант [beʃmant]	magic, milk
[n]	найза [najza]	name, normal
[ŋ]	булуң [buluŋ]	ring
[p]	пайдубал [pajdubal]	pencil, private
[r]	рахмат [raχmat]	rice, radio
[s]	сагызган [sagɪzgan]	city, boss
[ʃ]	бурулуш [buruluʃ]	machine, shark
[t]	түтүн [tytyn]	tourist, trip
[χ]	пахтадан [paχtadan]	hot, hobby
[ts]	шприц [ʃprits]	cats, tsetse fly
[tʃ]	биринчи [birintʃi]	church, French
[v]	квартал [kvartal]	very, river
[z]	казуу [kazuu]	zebra, please
[ʲ]	руль, актёр [rulʲ, aktʲor]	palatalization sign

ABBREVIATIONS
used in the vocabulary

English abbreviations

ab.	-	about
adj	-	adjective
adv	-	adverb
anim.	-	animate
as adj	-	attributive noun used as adjective
e.g.	-	for example
etc.	-	et cetera
fam.	-	familiar
fem.	-	feminine
form.	-	formal
inanim.	-	inanimate
masc.	-	masculine
math	-	mathematics
mil.	-	military
n	-	noun
pl	-	plural
pron.	-	pronoun
sb	-	somebody
sing.	-	singular
sth	-	something
v aux	-	auxiliary verb
vi	-	intransitive verb
vi, vt	-	intransitive, transitive verb
vt	-	transitive verb

BASIC CONCEPTS

Basic concepts. Part 1

1. Pronouns

I, me	мен, мага	men, maga
you	сен	sen
he, she, it	ал	al
we	биз	biz
you (to a group)	силер	siler
you (polite, sing.)	сиз	siz
you (polite, pl)	сиздер	sizder
they	алар	alar

2. Greetings. Salutations. Farewells

Hello! (fam.)	Салам!	salam!
Hello! (form.)	Саламатсызбы!	salamatsızbı!
Good morning!	Кутман таңыңыз менен!	kutman taŋıŋız menen!
Good afternoon!	Кутман күнүңүз менен!	kutman kynyŋyz menen!
Good evening!	Кутман кечиңиз менен!	kutman ketʃiŋiz menen!
to say hello	учурашуу	utʃuraʃuu
Hi! (hello)	Кандай!	kandaj!
greeting (n)	салам	salam
to greet (vt)	саламдашуу	salamdaʃuu
How are you?	Иштериң кандай?	iʃteriŋ kandaj?
How are you? (form.)	Иштериңиз кандай?	iʃteriŋiz kandaj?
How are you? (fam.)	Иштер кандай?	iʃter kandaj?
What's new?	Эмне жаңылык?	emne dʒaŋılık?
Bye-Bye! Goodbye!	Көрүшкөнчө!	køryʃkøntʃø!
See you soon!	Эмки жолукканга чейин!	emki dʒolukkanga tʃejin!
Farewell! (to a friend)	Кош бол!	koʃ bol!
Farewell! (form.)	кырк бир	kırk bir
to say goodbye	коштошуу	koʃtoʃuu
So long!	Жакшы кал!	dʒakʃı kal!
Thank you!	Рахмат!	raχmat!
Thank you very much!	Чоң рахмат!	tʃoŋ raχmat!

You're welcome	Эч нерсе эмес	etʃ nerse emes
Don't mention it!	Алкышка арзыбайт	alkıʃka arzıbajt
It was nothing	Эчтеке эмес.	etʃteke emes

Excuse me! (fam.)	Кечир!	ketʃir!
Excuse me! (form.)	Кечирип коюңузчу!	ketʃirip kojuŋuztʃu!
to excuse (forgive)	кечирүү	ketʃiryy

to apologize (vi)	кечирим суроо	ketʃirim suroo
My apologies	Кечирим сурайм.	ketʃirim surajm
I'm sorry!	Кечиресиз!	ketʃiresiz!
to forgive (vt)	кечирүү	ketʃiryy
It's okay! (that's all right)	Эч капачылык жок.	etʃ kapatʃılık dʒok
please (adv)	суранам	suranam

Don't forget!	Унутуп калбаңыз!	unutup kalbaŋız!
Certainly!	Албетте!	albette!
Of course not!	Албетте жок!	albette dʒok!
Okay! (I agree)	Макул!	makul!
That's enough!	Жетишет!	dʒetiʃet!

3. Cardinal numbers. Part 1

0 zero	нөл	nøl
1 one	бир	bir
2 two	эки	eki
3 three	үч	ytʃ
4 four	төрт	tørt

5 five	беш	beʃ
6 six	алты	altı
7 seven	жети	dʒeti
8 eight	сегиз	segiz
9 nine	тогуз	toguz

10 ten	он	on
11 eleven	он бир	on bir
12 twelve	он эки	on eki
13 thirteen	он үч	on ytʃ
14 fourteen	он төрт	on tørt

15 fifteen	он беш	on beʃ
16 sixteen	он алты	on altı
17 seventeen	он жети	on dʒeti
18 eighteen	он сегиз	on segiz
19 nineteen	он тогуз	on toguz

20 twenty	жыйырма	dʒıjırma
21 twenty-one	жыйырма бир	dʒıjırma bir
22 twenty-two	жыйырма эки	dʒıjırma eki

23 twenty-three	жыйырма үч	dʒıjırma ytʃ
30 thirty	отуз	otuz
31 thirty-one	отуз бир	otuz bir
32 thirty-two	отуз эки	otuz eki
33 thirty-three	отуз үч	otuz ytʃ
40 forty	кырк	kırk
42 forty-two	кырк эки	kırk eki
43 forty-three	кырк үч	kırk ytʃ
50 fifty	элүү	elyy
51 fifty-one	элүү бир	elyy bir
52 fifty-two	элүү эки	elyy eki
53 fifty-three	элүү үч	elyy ytʃ
60 sixty	алтымыш	altımıʃ
61 sixty-one	алтымыш бир	altımıʃ bir
62 sixty-two	алтымыш эки	altımıʃ eki
63 sixty-three	алтымыш үч	altımıʃ ytʃ
70 seventy	жетимиш	dʒetimiʃ
71 seventy-one	жетимиш бир	dʒetimiʃ bir
72 seventy-two	жетимиш эки	dʒetimiʃ eki
73 seventy-three	жетимиш үч	dʒetimiʃ ytʃ
80 eighty	сексен	seksen
81 eighty-one	сексен бир	seksen bir
82 eighty-two	сексен эки	seksen eki
83 eighty-three	сексен үч	seksen ytʃ
90 ninety	токсон	tokson
91 ninety-one	токсон бир	tokson bir
92 ninety-two	токсон эки	tokson eki
93 ninety-three	токсон үч	tokson ytʃ

4. Cardinal numbers. Part 2

100 one hundred	бир жүз	bir dʒyz
200 two hundred	эки жүз	eki dʒyz
300 three hundred	үч жүз	ytʃ dʒyz
400 four hundred	төрт жүз	tørt dʒyz
500 five hundred	беш жүз	beʃ dʒyz
600 six hundred	алты жүз	altı dʒyz
700 seven hundred	жети жүз	dʒeti dʒyz
800 eight hundred	сегиз жүз	segiz dʒyz
900 nine hundred	тогуз жүз	toguz dʒyz
1000 one thousand	бир миң	bir miŋ
2000 two thousand	эки миң	eki miŋ

3000 three thousand	үч миң	ytʃ miŋ
10000 ten thousand	он миң	on miŋ
one hundred thousand	жүз миң	dʒyz miŋ
million	миллион	million
billion	миллиард	milliard

5. Numbers. Fractions

fraction	бөлчөк	bøltʃøk
one half	экиден бир	ekiden bir
one third	үчтөн бир	ytʃtøn bir
one quarter	төрттөн бир	tørttøn bir
one eighth	сегизден бир	segizden bir
one tenth	тогуздан бир	toguzdan bir
two thirds	үчтөн эки	ytʃtøn eki
three quarters	төрттөн үч	tørttøn ytʃ

6. Numbers. Basic operations

subtraction	кемитүү	kemityy
to subtract (vi, vt)	кемитүү	kemityy
division	бөлүү	bølyy
to divide (vt)	бөлүү	bølyy
addition	кошуу	koʃuu
to add up (vt)	кошуу	koʃuu
to add (vi, vt)	кошуу	koʃuu
multiplication	көбөйтүү	købøjtyy
to multiply (vt)	көбөйтүү	købøjtyy

7. Numbers. Miscellaneous

digit, figure	санарип	sanarip
number	сан	san
numeral	сан атооч	san atootʃ
minus sign	кемитүү	kemityy
plus sign	плюс	plʉs
formula	формула	formula
calculation	эсептөө	eseptøø
to count (vi, vt)	саноо	sanoo
to count up	эсептөө	eseptøø
to compare (vt)	салыштыруу	salıʃtıruu
How much?	Канча?	kantʃa?
sum, total	жыйынтык	dʒıjıntık

| result | натыйжа | natıjʤa |
| remainder | калдык | kaldık |

a few (e.g., ~ years ago)	бир нече	bir netʃe
little (I had ~ time)	биртике	bir az
few (I have ~ friends)	бир аз	bir az
a little (~ water)	кичине	kitʃine
the rest	калганы	kalganı
one and a half	бир жарым	bir ʤarım
dozen	он эки даана	on eki daana

in half (adv)	тең экиге	teŋ ekige
equally (evenly)	тең	teŋ
half	жарым	ʤarım
time (three ~s)	бир жолу	bir ʤolu

8. The most important verbs. Part 1

to advise (vt)	кеңеш берүү	keŋeʃ beryy
to agree (say yes)	макул болуу	makul boluu
to answer (vi, vt)	жооп берүү	ʤoop beryy
to apologize (vi)	кечирим суроо	ketʃirim suroo
to arrive (vi)	келүү	kelyy

to ask (~ oneself)	суроо	suroo
to ask (~ sb to do sth)	суроо	suroo
to be (vi)	болуу	boluu

to be afraid	жазкануу	ʤazkanuu
to be hungry	ачка болуу	atʃka boluu
to be interested in ...	... кызыгуу	... kızıguu
to be needed	керек болуу	kerek boluu
to be surprised	таң калуу	taŋ kaluu

to be thirsty	суусап калуу	suusap kaluu
to begin (vt)	баштоо	baʃtoo
to belong to ...	таандык болуу	taandık boluu
to boast (vi)	мактануу	maktanuu
to break (split into pieces)	сындыруу	sındıruu

to call (~ for help)	чакыруу	tʃakıruu
can (v aux)	жасай алуу	ʤasai aluu
to catch (vt)	кармоо	karmoo
to change (vt)	өзгөртүү	øzgørtyy
to choose (select)	тандоо	tandoo

to come down (the stairs)	ылдый түшүү	ıldıj tyʃyy
to compare (vt)	салыштыруу	salıʃtıruu
to complain (vi, vt)	арыздануу	arızdanuu
to confuse (mix up)	адаштыруу	adaʃtıruu

| to continue (vt) | улантуу | ulantuu |
| to control (vt) | башкаруу | baʃkaruu |

to cook (dinner)	тамак бышыруу	tamak bıʃıruu
to cost (vt)	туруу	turuu
to count (add up)	саноо	sanoo
to count on ...	... ишенүү	... iʃenyy
to create (vt)	жаратуу	dʒaratuu
to cry (weep)	ыйлоо	ıjloo

9. The most important verbs. Part 2

to deceive (vi, vt)	алдоо	aldoo
to decorate (tree, street)	кооздоо	koozdoo
to defend (a country, etc.)	коргоо	korgoo
to demand (request firmly)	талап кылуу	talap kıluu
to dig (vt)	казуу	kazuu

to discuss (vt)	талкуулоо	talkuuloo
to do (vt)	кылуу	kıluu
to doubt (have doubts)	күмөн саноо	kymøn sanoo
to drop (let fall)	түшүрүп алуу	tyʃyryp aluu
to enter (room, house, etc.)	кирүү	kiryy

to excuse (forgive)	кечирүү	ketʃiryy
to exist (vi)	чыгуу	tʃıguu
to expect (foresee)	күтүү	kytyy
to explain (vt)	түшүндүрүү	tyʃyndyryy
to fall (vi)	жыгылуу	dʒıgıluu

to find (vt)	таап алуу	taap aluu
to finish (vt)	бүтүрүү	bytyryy
to fly (vi)	учуу	utʃuu
to follow ... (come after)	... ээрчүү	... eertʃyy
to forget (vi, vt)	унутуу	unutuu

to forgive (vt)	кечирүү	ketʃiryy
to give (vt)	берүү	beryy
to give a hint	четин чыгаруу	tʃetin tʃıgaruu
to go (on foot)	жөө басуу	dʒøø basuu

to go for a swim	сууга түшүү	suuga tyʃyy
to go out (for dinner, etc.)	чыгуу	tʃıguu
to guess (the answer)	жандырмагын табуу	dʒandırmagın tabuu

to have (vt)	бар болуу	bar boluu
to have breakfast	эртең менен тамактануу	erteŋ menen tamaktanuu
to have dinner	кечки тамакты ичүү	ketʃki tamaktı itʃyy

| to have lunch | түштөнүү | tyʃtønyy |
| to hear (vt) | угуу | uguu |

to help (vt)	жардам берүү	dʒardam beryy
to hide (vt)	жашынуу	dʒaʃınıı
to hope (vi, vt)	үмүттөнүү	ymyttønyy
to hunt (vi, vt)	аңчылык кылуу	aŋtʃılık kıluu
to hurry (vi)	шашуу	ʃaʃuu

10. The most important verbs. Part 3

to inform (vt)	маалымат берүү	maalımat beryy
to insist (vi, vt)	көшөрүү	køʃøryy
to insult (vt)	кемсинтүү	kemsintyy
to invite (vt)	чакыруу	tʃakıruu
to joke (vi)	тамашалоо	tamaʃaloo

to keep (vt)	сактоо	saktoo
to keep silent, to hush	унчукпоо	untʃukpoo
to kill (vt)	өлтүрүү	øltyryy
to know (sb)	таануу	taanuu
to know (sth)	билүү	bilyy
to laugh (vi)	күлүү	kylyy

to liberate (city, etc.)	бошотуу	boʃotuu
to like (I like …)	жактыруу	dʒaktıruu
to look for … (search)	… издөө	… izdøø
to love (sb)	сүйүү	syjyy
to make a mistake	ката кетирүү	kata ketiryy

to manage, to run	башкаруу	baʃkaruu
to mean (signify)	билдирүү	bildiryy
to mention (talk about)	айтып өтүү	ajtıp øtyy
to miss (school, etc.)	калтыруу	kaltıruu
to notice (see)	байкоо	bajkoo

to object (vi, vt)	каршы болуу	karʃı boluu
to observe (see)	байкоо салуу	bajkoo
to open (vt)	ачуу	atʃuu
to order (meal, etc.)	буйрутма кылуу	bujrutma kıluu
to order (mil.)	буйрук кылуу	bujruk kıluu
to own (possess)	ээ болуу	ee boluu

to participate (vi)	катышуу	katıʃuu
to pay (vi, vt)	төлөө	tøløø
to permit (vt)	уруксат берүү	uruksat beryy
to plan (vt)	пландаштыруу	plandaʃtıruu
to play (children)	ойноо	ojnoo
to pray (vi, vt)	дуба кылуу	duba kıluu
to prefer (vt)	артык көрүү	artık køryy

to promise (vt)	убада берүү	ubada beryy
to pronounce (vt)	айтуу	ajtuu
to propose (vt)	сунуштоо	sunuʃtoo
to punish (vt)	жазалоо	dʒazaloo

11. The most important verbs. Part 4

to read (vi, vt)	окуу	okuu
to recommend (vt)	сунуштоо	sunuʃtoo
to refuse (vi, vt)	баш тартуу	baʃ tartuu
to regret (be sorry)	өкүнүү	økynyy
to rent (sth from sb)	батирге алуу	batirge aluu

to repeat (say again)	кайталоо	kajtaloo
to reserve, to book	камдык буйрутмалоо	kamdık bujrutmaloo
to run (vi)	чуркоо	tʃurkoo
to save (rescue)	куткаруу	kutkaruu
to say (~ thank you)	айтуу	ajtuu

to scold (vt)	урушуу	uruʃuu
to see (vt)	көрүү	køryy
to sell (vt)	сатуу	satuu
to send (vt)	жөнөтүү	dʒønøtyy
to shoot (vi)	атуу	atuu

to shout (vi)	кыйкыруу	kıjkıruu
to show (vt)	көрсөтүү	kørsøtyy
to sign (document)	кол коюу	kol kojʉu
to sit down (vi)	отуруу	oturuu

to smile (vi)	жылмаюу	dʒılmadʒʉu
to speak (vi, vt)	сүйлөө	syjløø
to steal (money, etc.)	уурдоо	uurdoo
to stop (for pause, etc.)	токтоо	toktoo
to stop (please ~ calling me)	токтотуу	toktotuu

to study (vt)	окуу	okuu
to swim (vi)	сүзүү	syzyy
to take (vt)	алуу	aluu
to think (vi, vt)	ойлоо	ojloo
to threaten (vt)	коркутуу	korkutuu

to touch (with hands)	тийүү	tijyy
to translate (vt)	которуу	kotoruu
to trust (vt)	ишенүү	iʃenyy
to try (attempt)	аракет кылуу	araket kıluu
to turn (e.g., ~ left)	бурулуу	buruluu
to underestimate (vt)	баалабоо	baalaboo
to understand (vt)	түшүнүү	tyʃynyy

| to unite (vt) | бириктирүү | biriktiryy |
| to wait (vt) | күтүү | kytyy |

to want (wish, desire)	каалоо	kaaloo
to warn (vt)	эскертүү	eskertyy
to work (vi)	иштөө	iʃtøø
to write (vt)	жазуу	dʒazuu
to write down	кагазга түшүрүү	kagazga tyʃyryy

12. Colors

color	түс	tys
shade (tint)	кошумча түс	koʃumtʃa tys
hue	кубулуу	kubuluu
rainbow	күндүн кулагы	kyndyn kulagı

white (adj)	ак	ak
black (adj)	кара	kara
gray (adj)	боз	boz

green (adj)	жашыл	dʒaʃıl
yellow (adj)	сары	sarı
red (adj)	кызыл	kızıl

blue (adj)	көк	køk
light blue (adj)	көгүлтүр	køgyltyr
pink (adj)	мала	mala
orange (adj)	кызгылт сары	kızgılt sarı
violet (adj)	сыя көк	sıja køk
brown (adj)	күрөң	kyrøŋ

| golden (adj) | алтын түстүү | altın tystyy |
| silvery (adj) | күмүш өңдүү | kymyʃ øŋdyy |

beige (adj)	сары боз	sarı boz
cream (adj)	саргылт	sargılt
turquoise (adj)	бирюза	birɨza
cherry red (adj)	кочкул кызыл	kotʃkul kızıl
lilac (adj)	кызгылт көгүш	kızgılt køgyʃ
crimson (adj)	ачык кызыл	atʃık kızıl

light (adj)	ачык	atʃık
dark (adj)	күңүрт	kyŋyrt
bright, vivid (adj)	ачык	atʃık

colored (pencils)	түстүү	tystyy
color (e.g., ~ film)	түстүү	tystyy
black-and-white (adj)	ак-кара	ak-kara
plain (one-colored)	бир өңчөй түстө	bir øŋtʃøj tystø
multicolored (adj)	ар түрдүү түстө	ar tyrdyy tystø

13. Questions

Who?	Ким?	kim?
What?	Эмне?	emne?
Where? (at, in)	Каерде?	kaerde?
Where (to)?	Каяка?	kajaka?
From where?	Каяктан?	kajaktan?
When?	Качан?	katʃan?
Why? (What for?)	Эмне үчүн?	emne ytʃyn?
Why? (~ are you crying?)	Эмнеге?	emnege?

What for?	Кайсы керекке?	kajsı kerekke?
How? (in what way)	Кандай?	kandaj?
What? (What kind of ...?)	Кайсы?	kajsı?
Which?	Кайсынысы?	kajsınısı?

To whom?	Кимге?	kimge?
About whom?	Ким жөнүндө?	kim dʒønyndø?
About what?	Эмне жөнүндө?	emne dʒønyndø?
With whom?	Ким менен?	kim menen?

How many? How much?	Канча?	kantʃa?
Whose?	Кимдики?	kimdiki?
Whose? (fem.)	Кимдики?	kimdiki?
Whose? (pl)	Кимдердики?	kimderdiki?

14. Function words. Adverbs. Part 1

Where? (at, in)	Каерде?	kaerde?
here (adv)	бул жерде	bul dʒerde
there (adv)	тээтигил жакта	teetigil dʒakta

| somewhere (to be) | бир жерде | bir dʒerde |
| nowhere (not in any place) | эч жакта | etʃ dʒakta |

| by (near, beside) | ... жанында | ... dʒanında |
| by the window | терезенин жанында | terezenin dʒanında |

Where (to)?	Каяка?	kajaka?
here (e.g., come ~!)	бери	beri
there (e.g., to go ~)	нары	narı
from here (adv)	бул жерден	bul dʒerden
from there (adv)	тигил жерден	tigil dʒerden

| close (adv) | жакын | dʒakın |
| far (adv) | алыс | alıs |

| near (e.g., ~ Paris) | ... тегерегинде | ... tegereginde |
| nearby (adv) | жакын арада | dʒakın arada |

not far (adv)	алыс эмес	alıs emes
left (adj)	сол	sol
on the left	сол жакта	sol dʒakta
to the left	солго	solgo

right (adj)	оң	oŋ
on the right	оң жакта	oŋ dʒakta
to the right	оңго	oŋgo

in front (adv)	астыда	astıda
front (as adj)	алдыңкы	aldıŋkı
ahead (the kids ran ~)	алдыга	aldıga

behind (adv)	артында	artında
from behind	артынан	artınan
back (towards the rear)	артка	artka

| middle | ортосу | ortosu |
| in the middle | ортосунда | ortosunda |

at the side	капталында	kaptalında
everywhere (adv)	бүт жерде	byt dʒerde
around (in all directions)	айланасында	ajlanasında

from inside	ичинде	itʃinde
somewhere (to go)	бир жерде	bir dʒerde
straight (directly)	түз	tyz
back (e.g., come ~)	кайра	kajra

| from anywhere | бир жерден | bir dʒerden |
| from somewhere | бир жактан | bir dʒaktan |

firstly (adv)	биринчиден	birintʃiden
secondly (adv)	экинчиден	ekintʃiden
thirdly (adv)	үчүнчүдөн	ytʃyntʃydøn

suddenly (adv)	күтпөгөн жерден	kytpøgøn dʒerden
at first (in the beginning)	башында	baʃında
for the first time	биринчи жолу	birintʃi dʒolu
long before ...	... алдында	... aldında
anew (over again)	башынан	baʃınan
for good (adv)	түбөлүккө	tybølykkø

never (adv)	эч качан	etʃ katʃan
again (adv)	кайра	kajra
now (at present)	эми	emi
often (adv)	көпчүлүк учурда	køptʃylyk utʃurda
then (adv)	анда	anda
urgently (quickly)	тезинен	tezinen
usually (adv)	көбүнчө	købyntʃø
by the way, ...	баса, ...	basa, ...
possibly	мүмкүн	mymkyn

probably (adv)	балким	balkim
maybe (adv)	ыктымал	ıktımal
besides ...	андан тышкары, ...	andan tıʃkarı, ...
that's why ...	ошондуктан ...	oʃonduktan ...
in spite of ...	... карабастан	... karabastan
thanks to ...	... күчү менен	... kytʃy menen

what (pron.)	эмне	emne
that (conj.)	эмне	emne
something	бир нерсе	bir nerse
anything (something)	бир нерсе	bir nerse
nothing	эч нерсе	etʃ nerse

who (pron.)	ким	kim
someone	кимдир бирөө	kimdir birøø
somebody	бирөө жарым	birøø dʒarım

nobody	эч ким	etʃ kim
nowhere (a voyage to ~)	эч жака	etʃ dʒaka
nobody's	эч кимдики	etʃ kimdiki
somebody's	бирөөнүкү	birøønyky

so (I'm ~ glad)	эми	emi
also (as well)	ошондой эле	oʃondoj ele
too (as well)	дагы	dagı

15. Function words. Adverbs. Part 2

Why?	Эмнеге?	emnege?
for some reason	эмнегедир	emnegedir
because ...	... себептен	... sebepten
for some purpose	эмне үчүндүр	emne ytʃyndyr

and	жана	dʒana
or	же	dʒe
but	бирок	birok
for (e.g., ~ me)	үчүн	ytʃyn

too (~ many people)	өтө эле	øtø ele
only (exclusively)	азыр эле	azır ele
exactly (adv)	так	tak
about (more or less)	болжол менен	boldʒol menen

approximately (adv)	болжол менен	boldʒol menen
approximate (adj)	болжолдуу	boldʒolduu
almost (adv)	дээрлик	deerlik
the rest	калганы	kalganı

| the other (second) | башка | baʃka |
| other (different) | башка бөлөк | baʃka bøløk |

each (adj)	ар бири	ar biri
any (no matter which)	баардык	baardık
many, much (a lot of)	көп	køp
many people	көбү	køby
all (everyone)	баары	baarı

in return for ...	... алмашуу	... almaʃuu
in exchange (adv)	ордуна	orduna
by hand (made)	колго	kolgo
hardly (negative opinion)	ишенүүгө болбойт	iʃenyygø bolbojt

probably (adv)	балким	balkim
on purpose (intentionally)	атайын	atajın
by accident (adv)	кокустан	kokustan

very (adv)	аябай	ajabaj
for example (adv)	мисалы	misalı
between	ортосунда	ortosunda
among	арасында	arasında
so much (such a lot)	ошончо	oʃontʃo
especially (adv)	өзгөчө	øzgøtʃø

Basic concepts. Part 2

16. Weekdays

Monday	дүйшөмбү	dyjʃømby
Tuesday	шейшемби	ʃejʃembi
Wednesday	шаршемби	ʃarʃembi
Thursday	бейшемби	bejʃembi
Friday	жума	ʤuma
Saturday	ишенби	iʃenbi
Sunday	жекшемби	ʤekʃembi

today (adv)	бүгүн	bygyn
tomorrow (adv)	эртең	erteŋ
the day after tomorrow	бирсүгүнү	birsygyny
yesterday (adv)	кечээ	ketʃee
the day before yesterday	мурда күнү	murda kyny

day	күн	kyn
working day	иш күнү	iʃ kyny
public holiday	майрам күнү	majram kyny
day off	дем алыш күн	dem alıʃ kyn
weekend	дем алыш күндөр	dem alıʃ kyndør

all day long	күнү бою	kyny boju
the next day (adv)	кийинки күнү	kijinki kyny
two days ago	эки күн мурун	eki kyn murun
the day before	жакында	ʤakında
daily (adj)	күндө	kyndø
every day (adv)	күн сайын	kyn sajın

week	жума	ʤuma
last week (adv)	өткөн жумада	øtkøn ʤumada
next week (adv)	келаткан жумада	kelatkan ʤumada
weekly (adj)	жума сайын	ʤuma sajın
every week (adv)	жума сайын	ʤuma sajın
twice a week	жумасына эки жолу	ʤumasına eki ʤolu
every Tuesday	ар шейшемби	ar ʃejʃembi

17. Hours. Day and night

morning	таң	taŋ
in the morning	эртең менен	erteŋ menen
noon, midday	жарым күн	ʤarım kyn

in the afternoon	түштөн кийин	tyʃtøn kijin
evening	кеч	ketʃ
in the evening	кечинде	ketʃinde
night	түн	tyn
at night	түндө	tyndø
midnight	жарым түн	dʒarım tyn

second	секунда	sekunda
minute	мүнөт	mynøt
hour	саат	saat
half an hour	жарым саат	dʒarım saat
a quarter-hour	чейрек саат	tʃejrek saat
fifteen minutes	он беш мүнөт	on beʃ mynøt
24 hours	сутка	sutka

sunrise	күндүн чыгышы	kyndyn tʃıgıʃı
dawn	таң агаруу	taŋ agaruu
early morning	таң эрте	taŋ erte
sunset	күн батуу	kyn batuu

early in the morning	таң эрте	taŋ erte
this morning	бүгүн эртең менен	bygyn erteŋ menen
tomorrow morning	эртең эртең менен	erteŋ erteŋ menen

this afternoon	күндүзү	kyndyzy
in the afternoon	түштөн кийин	tyʃtøn kijin
tomorrow afternoon	эртең түштөн кийин	erteŋ tyʃtøn kijin

| tonight (this evening) | бүгүн кечинде | bygyn ketʃinde |
| tomorrow night | эртең кечинде | erteŋ ketʃinde |

at 3 o'clock sharp	туура саат үчтө	tuura saat ytʃtø
about 4 o'clock	болжол менен төрт саат	boldʒol menen tørt saat
by 12 o'clock	саат он экиде	saat on ekide

in 20 minutes	жыйырма мүнөттөн кийин	dʒıjırma mynøttøn kijin
in an hour	бир сааттан кийин	bir saattan kijin
on time (adv)	өз убагында	øz ubagında

a quarter to ...	... он беш мүнөт калды	... on beʃ mynøt kaldı
within an hour	бир сааттын ичинде	bir saattın itʃinde
every 15 minutes	он беш мүнөт сайын	on beʃ mynøt sajın
round the clock	бир сутка бою	bir sutka bojʉ

18. Months. Seasons

| January | январь | janvarʲ |
| February | февраль | fevralʲ |

March	март	mart
April	апрель	aprelʲ
May	май	maj
June	июнь	ijʉnʲ

July	июль	ijʉlʲ
August	август	avgust
September	сентябрь	sentʲabrʲ
October	октябрь	oktʲabrʲ
November	ноябрь	nojabrʲ
December	декабрь	dekabrʲ

spring	жаз	dʒaz
in spring	жазында	dʒazında
spring (as adj)	жазгы	dʒazgı

summer	жай	dʒaj
in summer	жайында	dʒajında
summer (as adj)	жайкы	dʒajkı

fall	күз	kyz
in fall	күзүндө	kyzyndø
fall (as adj)	күздүк	kyzdyk

winter	кыш	kıʃ
in winter	кышында	kıʃında
winter (as adj)	кышкы	kıʃkı

month	ай	aj
this month	ушул айда	uʃul ajda
next month	кийинки айда	kijinki ajda
last month	өткөн айда	øtkøn ajda

a month ago	бир ай мурун	bir aj murun
in a month (a month later)	бир айдан кийин	bir ajdan kijin
in 2 months (2 months later)	эки айдан кийин	eki ajdan kijin
the whole month	ай бою	aj bojʉ
all month long	толук бир ай	toluk bir aj

monthly (~ magazine)	ай сайын	aj sajın
monthly (adv)	ай сайын	aj sajın
every month	ар бир айда	ar bir ajda
twice a month	айына эки жолу	ajına eki dʒolu

year	жыл	dʒıl
this year	бул жылы	bul dʒılı
next year	келаткан жылы	kelatkan dʒılı
last year	өткөн жылы	øtkøn dʒılı

| a year ago | бир жыл мурун | bir dʒıl murun |
| in a year | бир жылдан кийин | bir dʒıldan kijin |

in two years	эки жылдан кийин	eki dʒıldan kijin
the whole year	жыл бою	dʒıl bodʒʉ
all year long	толук бир жыл	toluk bir dʒıl

every year	жыл сайын	dʒıl sajın
annual (adj)	жыл сайын	dʒıl sajın
annually (adv)	жыл сайын	dʒıl sajın
4 times a year	жылына төрт жолу	dʒılına tørt dʒolu

date (e.g., today's ~)	число	tʃislo
date (e.g., ~ of birth)	күн	kyn
calendar	календарь	kalendarʲ

half a year	жарым жыл	dʒarım dʒıl
six months	жарым чейрек	dʒarım tʃejrek
season (summer, etc.)	мезгил	mezgil
century	кылым	kılım

19. Time. Miscellaneous

time	убакыт	ubakıt
moment	учур	utʃur
instant (n)	көз ирмемде	køz irmemde
instant (adj)	көз ирмемде	køz irmemde
lapse (of time)	убакыттын бир бөлүгү	ubakıttın bir bølygy
life	жашоо	dʒaʃoo
eternity	түбөлүк	tybølyk

epoch	доор	door
era	заман	zaman
cycle	мерчим	mertʃim
period	мезгил	mezgil
term (short-~)	мөөнөт	møønøt

the future	келечек	keletʃek
future (as adj)	келечек	keletʃek
next time	кийинки жолу	kijinki dʒolu
the past	өткөн	øtkøn
past (recent)	өткөн	øtkøn
last time	өткөндө	øtkøndø

later (adv)	кийнчерээк	kijntʃereek
after (prep.)	кийин	kijin
nowadays (adv)	азыр, учурда	azır, utʃurda
now (at this moment)	азыр	azır
immediately (adv)	тез арада	tez arada
soon (adv)	жакында	dʒakında
in advance (beforehand)	алдын ала	aldın ala
a long time ago	көп убакыт мурун	køp ubakıt murun
recently (adv)	жакындан бери	dʒakından beri

destiny	тагдыр	tagdır
memories (childhood ~)	эсте калганы	este kalganı
archives	архив	arχiv

during ...	... убагында	... ubagında
long, a long time (adv)	узак	uzak
not long (adv)	узак эмес	uzak emes
early (in the morning)	эрте	erte
late (not early)	кеч	ketʃ

forever (for good)	түбөлүк	tybølyk
to start (begin)	баштоо	baʃtoo
to postpone (vt)	жылдыруу	dʒıldıruu

at the same time	бир учурда	bir utʃurda
permanently (adv)	үзгүлтүксүз	yzgyltyksyz
constant (noise, pain)	үзгүлтүксүз	yzgyltyksyz
temporary (adj)	убактылуу	ubaktıluu

sometimes (adv)	кедээ	kedee
rarely (adv)	чанда	tʃanda
often (adv)	көпчүлүк учурда	køptʃylyk utʃurda

20. Opposites

| rich (adj) | бай | baj |
| poor (adj) | кедей | kedej |

| ill, sick (adj) | оорулуу | ooruluu |
| well (not sick) | дени сак | deni sak |

| big (adj) | чоң | tʃoŋ |
| small (adj) | кичине | kitʃine |

| quickly (adv) | тез | tez |
| slowly (adv) | жай | dʒaj |

| fast (adj) | тез | tez |
| slow (adj) | жай | dʒaj |

| glad (adj) | шайыр | ʃajır |
| sad (adj) | муңдуу | muŋduu |

| together (adv) | бирге | birge |
| separately (adv) | өзүнчө | øzyntʃø |

aloud (to read)	үн чыгарып	yn tʃıgarıp
silently (to oneself)	үн чыгарбай	yn tʃıgarbaj
tall (adj)	бийик	bijik
low (adj)	жапыз	dʒapız

| deep (adj) | терең | tereŋ |
| shallow (adj) | тайыз | tajız |

| yes | ооба | ooba |
| no | жок | dʒok |

| distant (in space) | алыс | alıs |
| nearby (adj) | жакын | dʒakın |

| far (adv) | алыс | alıs |
| nearby (adv) | жакын арада | dʒakın arada |

| long (adj) | узун | uzun |
| short (adj) | кыска | kıska |

| good (kindhearted) | кайрымдуу | kajrımduu |
| evil (adj) | каардуу | kaarduu |

| married (adj) | аялы бар | ajalı bar |
| single (adj) | бойдок | bojdok |

| to forbid (vt) | тыюу салуу | tıjʉu saluu |
| to permit (vt) | уруксат берүү | uruksat beryy |

| end | аягы | ajagı |
| beginning | башталыш | baʃtalıʃ |

| left (adj) | сол | sol |
| right (adj) | оң | oŋ |

| first (adj) | биринчи | birintʃi |
| last (adj) | акыркы | akırkı |

| crime | кылмыш | kılmıʃ |
| punishment | жаза | dʒaza |

| to order (vt) | буйрук кылуу | bujruk kıluu |
| to obey (vi, vt) | баш ийүү | baʃ ijyy |

| straight (adj) | түз | tyz |
| curved (adj) | кыйшак | kıʃʃak |

| paradise | бейиш | bejiʃ |
| hell | тозок | tozok |

| to be born | төрөлүү | tørølyy |
| to die (vi) | өлүү | ølyy |

strong (adj)	күчтүү	kytʃtyy
weak (adj)	алсыз	alsız
old (adj)	эски	eski
young (adj)	жаш	dʒaʃ

| old (adj) | эски | eski |
| new (adj) | жаңы | dʒaŋɪ |

| hard (adj) | катуу | katuu |
| soft (adj) | жумшак | dʒumʃak |

| warm (tepid) | жылуу | dʒɪluu |
| cold (adj) | муздак | muzdak |

| fat (adj) | семиз | semiz |
| thin (adj) | арык | arɪk |

| narrow (adj) | тар | tar |
| wide (adj) | кең | keŋ |

| good (adj) | жакшы | dʒakʃɪ |
| bad (adj) | жаман | dʒaman |

| brave (adj) | кайраттуу | kajrattuu |
| cowardly (adj) | суу жүрөк | suu dʒyrøk |

21. Lines and shapes

square	чарчы	tʃartʃɪ
square (as adj)	чарчы	tʃartʃɪ
circle	тегерек	tegerek
round (adj)	тегерек	tegerek
triangle	үч бурчтук	ytʃ burtʃtuk
triangular (adj)	үч бурчтуу	ytʃ burtʃtuu

oval	жумуру	dʒumuru
oval (as adj)	жумуру	dʒumuru
rectangle	тик бурчтук	tik burtʃtuk
rectangular (adj)	тик бурчтуу	tik burtʃtuu

pyramid	пирамида	piramida
rhombus	ромб	romb
trapezoid	трапеция	trapetsija
cube	куб	kub
prism	призма	prizma

circumference	айлана	ajlana
sphere	сфера	sfera
ball (solid sphere)	шар	ʃar
diameter	диаметр	diametr
radius	радиус	radius
perimeter (circle's ~)	периметр	perimetr
center	борбор	borbor
horizontal (adj)	туурасынан	tuurasɪnan
vertical (adj)	тикесинен	tikesinen

| parallel (n) | параллель | parallelʲ |
| parallel (as adj) | параллель | parallelʲ |

line	сызык	sɪzɪk
stroke	сызык	sɪzɪk
straight line	түз сызык	tyz sɪzɪk
curve (curved line)	кыйшык сызык	kɪjʃɪk sɪzɪk
thin (line, etc.)	ичке	itʃke
contour (outline)	караан	karaan

intersection	кесилиш	kesiliʃ
right angle	тик бурч	tik burtʃ
segment	сегмент	segment
sector (circular ~)	сектор	sektor
side (of triangle)	каптал	kaptal
angle	бурч	burtʃ

22. Units of measurement

weight	салмак	salmak
length	узундук	uzunduk
width	жазылык	dʒazɪlɪk
height	бийиктик	bijiktik
depth	терендик	terendik
volume	көлөм	køløm
area	аянт	ajant

gram	грамм	gramm
milligram	миллиграмм	milligramm
kilogram	килограмм	kilogramm
ton	тонна	tonna
pound	фунт	funt
ounce	унция	untsija

meter	метр	metr
millimeter	миллиметр	millimetr
centimeter	сантиметр	santimetr
kilometer	километр	kilometr
mile	миля	milʲa

inch	дюйм	dʉjm
foot	фут	fut
yard	ярд	jard

| square meter | квадраттык метр | kvadrattɪk metr |
| hectare | гектар | gektar |

liter	литр	litr
degree	градус	gradus
volt	вольт	volʲt

ampere	эмпер	amper
horsepower	ат күчү	at kytʃy
quantity	саны	sanı
a little bit of ...	... бир аз	... bir az
half	жарым	dʒarım
dozen	он эки даана	on eki daana
piece (item)	даана	daana
size	чоңдук	tʃoŋduk
scale (map ~)	өлчөмчен	øltʃømtʃen
minimal (adj)	минималдуу	minimalduu
the smallest (adj)	эң кичинекей	eŋ kitʃinekej
medium (adj)	орточо	ortotʃo
maximal (adj)	максималдуу	maksimalduu
the largest (adj)	эң чоң	eŋ tʃoŋ

23. Containers

canning jar (glass ~)	банка	banka
can	банка	banka
bucket	чака	tʃaka
barrel	бочка	botʃka
wash basin (e.g., plastic ~)	дагара	dagara
tank (100L water ~)	бак	bak
hip flask	фляжка	flʲadʒka
jerrycan	канистра	kanistra
tank (e.g., tank car)	цистерна	tsısterna
mug	кружка	krudʒka
cup (of coffee, etc.)	чөйчөк	tʃøjtʃøk
saucer	табак	tabak
glass (tumbler)	ыстакан	ıstakan
wine glass	бокал	bokal
stock pot (soup pot)	мискей	miskej
bottle (~ of wine)	бөтөлкө	bøtølkø
neck (of the bottle, etc.)	оозу	oozu
carafe (decanter)	графин	grafin
pitcher	кумура	kumura
vessel (container)	идиш	idiʃ
pot (crock, stoneware ~)	карапа	karapa
vase	ваза	vaza
flacon, bottle (perfume ~)	флакон	flakon
vial, small bottle	кичине бөтөлкө	kitʃine bøtølkø

tube (of toothpaste)	тюбик	tʉbik
sack (bag)	кап	kap
bag (paper ~, plastic ~)	пакет	paket
pack (of cigarettes, etc.)	пачке	patʃke
box (e.g., shoebox)	куту	kutu
crate	үкөк	ykøk
basket	себет	sebet

24. Materials

material	материал	material
wood (n)	жыгач	dʒɪgatʃ
wood-, wooden (adj)	жыгач	dʒɪgatʃ
glass (n)	айнек	ajnek
glass (as adj)	айнек	ajnek
stone (n)	таш	taʃ
stone (as adj)	таш	taʃ
plastic (n)	пластик	plastik
plastic (as adj)	пластик	plastik
rubber (n)	резина	rezina
rubber (as adj)	резина	rezina
cloth, fabric (n)	кездеме	kezdeme
fabric (as adj)	кездеме	kezdeme
paper (n)	кагаз	kagaz
paper (as adj)	кагаз	kagaz
cardboard (n)	картон	karton
cardboard (as adj)	картон	karton
polyethylene	полиэтилен	polietilen
cellophane	целлофан	tsellofan
linoleum	линолеум	linoleum
plywood	фанера	fanera
porcelain (n)	фарфор	farfor
porcelain (as adj)	фарфор	farfor
clay (n)	чопо	tʃopo
clay (as adj)	чопо	tʃopo
ceramic (n)	карапа	karapa
ceramic (as adj)	карапа	karapa

25. Metals

metal (n)	металл	metall
metal (as adj)	металл	metall
alloy (n)	эритме	eritme
gold (n)	алтын	altın
gold, golden (adj)	алтын	altın
silver (n)	күмүш	kymyʃ
silver (as adj)	күмүш	kymyʃ
iron (n)	темир	temir
iron-, made of iron (adj)	темир	temir
steel (n)	болот	bolot
steel (as adj)	болот	bolot
copper (n)	жез	dʒez
copper (as adj)	жез	dʒez
aluminum (n)	алюминий	alʉminij
aluminum (as adj)	алюминий	alʉminij
bronze (n)	коло	kolo
bronze (as adj)	коло	kolo
brass	латунь	latunʲ
nickel	никель	nikelʲ
platinum	платина	platina
mercury	сымап	sımap
tin	калай	kalaj
lead	коргошун	korgoʃun
zinc	цинк	tsınk

HUMAN BEING

Human being. The body

26. Humans. Basic concepts

human being	адам	adam
man (adult male)	эркек	erkek
woman	аял	ajal
child	бала	bala
girl	кыз бала	kız bala
boy	бала	bala
teenager	өспүрүм	øspyrym
old man	абышка	abıʃka
old woman	кемпир	kempir

27. Human anatomy

organism (body)	организм	organizm
heart	жүрөк	dʒyrøk
blood	кан	kan
artery	артерия	arterija
vein	вена	vena
brain	мээ	mee
nerve	нерв	nerv
nerves	нервдер	nervder
vertebra	омуртка	omurtka
spine (backbone)	кыр арка	kır arka
stomach (organ)	ашказан	aʃkazan
intestines, bowels	ичеги-карын	itʃegi-karın
intestine (e.g., large ~)	ичеги	itʃegi
liver	боор	boor
kidney	бөйрөк	bøjrøk
bone	сөөк	søøk
skeleton	скелет	skelet
rib	кабырга	kabırga
skull	баш сөөгү	baʃ søøgy
muscle	булчуң	bultʃuŋ
biceps	бицепс	bitseps

triceps	трицепс	tritseps
tendon	тарамыш	taramıʃ
joint	муундар	muundar
lungs	өпкө	øpkø
genitals	жан жер	dʒan dʒer
skin	тери	teri

28. Head

head	баш	baʃ
face	бет	bet
nose	мурун	murun
mouth	ооз	ooz

eye	көз	køz
eyes	көздөр	køzdør
pupil	карек	karek
eyebrow	каш	kaʃ
eyelash	кирпик	kirpik
eyelid	кабак	kabak

tongue	тил	til
tooth	тиш	tiʃ
lips	эриндер	erinder
cheekbones	бет сөөгү	bet søøgy
gum	тиш эти	tiʃ eti
palate	таңдай	taŋdaj

nostrils	мурун тешиги	murun teʃigi
chin	ээк	eek
jaw	жаак	dʒaak
cheek	бет	bet

forehead	чеке	tʃeke
temple	чыкый	tʃıkıj
ear	кулак	kulak
back of the head	желке	dʒelke
neck	моюн	mojʉn
throat	тамак	tamak

hair	чач	tʃatʃ
hairstyle	чач жасоо	tʃatʃ dʒasoo
haircut	чач кыркуу	tʃatʃ kırkuu
wig	парик	parik

mustache	мурут	murut
beard	сакал	sakal
to have (a beard, etc.)	мурут коюу	murut kojʉu
braid	өрүм чач	ørym tʃatʃ
sideburns	бакенбарда	bakenbarda

red-haired (adj)	сары	sarı
gray (hair)	ак чачтуу	ak tʃatʃtuu
bald (adj)	таз	taz
bald patch	кашка	kaʃka
ponytail	куйрук	kujruk
bangs	көкүл	køkyl

29. Human body

hand	беш манжа	beʃ mandʒa
arm	кол	kol
finger	манжа	mandʒa
toe	манжа	mandʒa
thumb	бармак	barmak
little finger	чыпалак	tʃıpalak
nail	тырмак	tırmak
fist	муштум	muʃtum
palm	алакан	alakan
wrist	билек	bilek
forearm	каруу	karuu
elbow	чыканак	tʃikanak
shoulder	ийин	ijin
leg	бут	but
foot	таман	taman
knee	тизе	tize
calf (part of leg)	балтыр	baltır
hip	сан	san
heel	согончок	sogontʃok
body	дене	dene
stomach	курсак	kursak
chest	төш	tøʃ
breast	эмчек	emtʃek
flank	каптал	kaptal
back	арка жон	arka dʒon
lower back	бел	bel
waist	бел	bel
navel (belly button)	киндик	kindik
buttocks	жамбаш	dʒambaʃ
bottom	көчүк	køtʃyk
beauty mark	мең	meŋ
birthmark	кал	kal
(café au lait spot)		
tattoo	татуировка	tatuirovka
scar	тырык	tırık

Clothing & Accessories

30. Outerwear. Coats

clothes	кийим	kijim
outerwear	үстүнкү кийим	ystyŋky kijim
winter clothing	кышкы кийим	kıʃkı kijim
coat (overcoat)	пальто	palʲto
fur coat	тон	ton
fur jacket	чолок тон	ʧolok ton
down coat	мамык олпок	mamık olpok
jacket (e.g., leather ~)	күрмө	kyrmø
raincoat (trenchcoat, etc.)	плащ	plaʃʧ
waterproof (adj)	суу өткүс	suu øtkys

31. Men's & women's clothing

shirt (button shirt)	көйнөк	køjnøk
pants	шым	ʃım
jeans	джинсы	dʒinsı
suit jacket	бешмант	beʃmant
suit	костюм	kostɯm
dress (frock)	көйнөк	køjnøk
skirt	юбка	jɯbka
blouse	блузка	bluzka
knitted jacket (cardigan, etc.)	кофта	kofta
jacket (of woman's suit)	кыска бешмант	kıska beʃmant
T-shirt	футболка	futbolka
shorts (short trousers)	чолок шым	ʧolok ʃım
tracksuit	спорт кийими	sport kijimi
bathrobe	халат	χalat
pajamas	пижама	pidʒama
sweater	свитер	sviter
pullover	пуловер	pulover
vest	жилет	dʒilet
tailcoat	фрак	frak
tuxedo	смокинг	smoking

uniform	форма	forma
workwear	жумуш кийим	ʤumuʃ kijim
overalls	комбинезон	kombinezon
coat (e.g., doctor's smock)	халат	χalat

32. Clothing. Underwear

underwear	ич кийим	iʧ kijim
boxers, briefs	эркектер чолок дамбалы	erkekter ʧolok dambalı
panties	аялдар трусиги	ajaldar trusigi
undershirt (A-shirt)	майка	majka
socks	байпак	bajpak
nightdress	жатаарда кийүүчү көйнөк	ʤataarda kijyyʧy køjnøk
bra	бюстгальтер	bʉstgalʲter
knee highs (knee-high socks)	гольфы	golʲfı
pantyhose	колготки	kolgotki
stockings (thigh highs)	байпак	bajpak
bathing suit	купальник	kupalʲnik

33. Headwear

hat	топу	topu
fedora	шляпа	ʃlʲapa
baseball cap	бейсболка	bejsbolka
flatcap	кепка	kepka
beret	берет	beret
hood	капюшон	kapʉʃon
panama hat	панамка	panamka
knit cap (knitted hat)	токулган шапка	tokulgan ʃapka
headscarf	жоолук	ʤooluk
women's hat	шляпа	ʃlʲapa
hard hat	каска	kaska
garrison cap	пилотка	pilotka
helmet	шлем	ʃlem
derby	котелок	kotelok
top hat	цилиндр	ʦılindr

34. Footwear

footwear	бут кийим	but kijim
shoes (men's shoes)	ботинка	botinka
shoes (women's shoes)	туфли	tufli
boots (e.g., cowboy ~)	өтүк	øtyk
slippers	тапочка	tapotʃka

tennis shoes (e.g., Nike ~)	кроссовка	krossovka
sneakers (e.g., Converse ~)	кеды	kedɪ
sandals	сандалии	sandalii

cobbler (shoe repairer)	өтүкчү	øtyktʃy
heel	така	taka
pair (of shoes)	түгөй	tygøj

shoestring	боо	boo
to lace (vt)	боолоо	booloo
shoehorn	кашык	kaʃik
shoe polish	өтүк май	øtyk maj

35. Textile. Fabrics

cotton (n)	пахта	paχta
cotton (as adj)	пахтадан	paχtadan
flax (n)	зыгыр	zɪgɪr
flax (as adj)	зыгырдан	zɪgɪrdan

| silk (n) | жибек | dʒibek |
| silk (as adj) | жибек | dʒibek |

| wool (n) | жүн | dʒyn |
| wool (as adj) | жүндөн | dʒyndøn |

velvet	баркыт	barkɪt
suede	күдөрү	kydøry
corduroy	чий баркыт	tʃij barkɪt

| nylon (n) | нейлон | nejlon |
| nylon (as adj) | нейлон | nejlon |

| polyester (n) | полиэстер | poliester |
| polyester (as adj) | полиэстер | poliester |

leather (n)	булгаары	bulgaarɪ
leather (as adj)	булгаары	bulgaarɪ
fur (n)	тери	teri
fur (e.g., ~ coat)	тери	teri

36. Personal accessories

gloves	колкап	kolkap
mittens	мээлэй	mæælæj
scarf (muffler)	моюн орогуч	mojun orogutʃ
glasses (eyeglasses)	көз айнек	køz ajnek
frame (eyeglass ~)	алкак	alkak
umbrella	чатырча	tʃatırtʃa
walking stick	аса таяк	asa tajak
hairbrush	тарак	tarak
fan	желпингич	dʒelpingitʃ
tie (necktie)	галстук	galstuk
bow tie	галстук-бабочка	galstuk-babotʃka
suspenders	шым тарткыч	ʃım tartkıtʃ
handkerchief	бетаарчы	betaartʃı
comb	тарак	tarak
barrette	чачсайгы	tʃatʃsajgı
hairpin	шпилька	ʃpilʲka
buckle	таралга	taralga
belt	кайыш кур	kajıʃ kur
shoulder strap	илгич	ilgitʃ
bag (handbag)	колбаштык	kolbaʃtık
purse	кичине колбаштык	kitʃine kolbaʃtık
backpack	жонбаштык	dʒonbaʃtık

37. Clothing. Miscellaneous

fashion	мода	moda
in vogue (adj)	саркеч	sarketʃ
fashion designer	модельер	modeljer
collar	жака	dʒaka
pocket	чөнтөк	tʃøntøk
pocket (as adj)	чөнтөк	tʃøntøk
sleeve	жең	dʒeŋ
hanging loop	илгич	ilgitʃ
fly (on trousers)	ширинка	ʃirinka
zipper (fastener)	молния	molnija
fastener	топчулук	toptʃuluk
button	топчу	toptʃu
buttonhole	илмек	ilmek
to come off (ab. button)	үзүлүү	yzylyy
to sew (vi, vt)	тигүү	tigyy

to embroider (vi, vt)	сайм**а** сайуу	sajma sajuu
embroidery	сайма	sajma
sewing needle	ийне	ijne
thread	жип	dʒip
seam	тигиш	tigiʃ

to get dirty (vi)	булгап алуу	bulgap aluu
stain (mark, spot)	так	tak
to crease, crumple (vi)	бырышып калуу	bırıʃıp kaluu
to tear, to rip (vt)	айрылуу	ajrıluu
clothes moth	күбө	kybø

38. Personal care. Cosmetics

toothpaste	тиш пастасы	tiʃ pastası
toothbrush	тиш щёткасы	tiʃ ʃtʃotkası
to brush one's teeth	тиш жуу	tiʃ dʒuu

razor	устара	ustara
shaving cream	кырынуу үчүн көбүк	kırınuu ytʃyn købyk
to shave (vi)	кырынуу	kırınuu

| soap | самын | samın |
| shampoo | шампунь | ʃampunʲ |

scissors	кайчы	kajtʃı
nail file	тырмак өгөө	tırmak øgøø
nail clippers	тырмак кычкачы	tırmak kıtʃkatʃı
tweezers	искек	iskek

cosmetics	упа-эндик	upa-endik
face mask	маска	maska
manicure	маникюр	manikʉr
to have a manicure	маникюр жасоо	manikdʒʉr dʒasoo
pedicure	педикюр	pedikʉr

make-up bag	косметичка	kosmetitʃka
face powder	упа	upa
powder compact	упа кутусу	upa kutusu
blusher	эндик	endik

perfume (bottled)	атыр	atır
toilet water (lotion)	туалет атыр суусу	tualet atır suusu
lotion	лосьон	losʲon
cologne	одеколон	odekolon

eyeshadow	көз боёгу	køz bojogu
eyeliner	көз карандашы	køz karandaʃı
mascara	кирпик үчүн боек	kirpik ytʃyn boek
lipstick	эрин помадасы	erin pomadası

nail polish, enamel	тырмак үчүн лак	tırmak ytʃyn lak
hair spray	чач үчүн лак	ʧatʃ ytʃyn lak
deodorant	дезодорант	dezodorant
cream	крем	krem
face cream	бетмай	betmaj
hand cream	кол үчүн май	kol ytʃyn maj
anti-wrinkle cream	бырыштарга каршы бет май	bırıʃtarga karʃı bet maj
day cream	күндүзгү бет май	kyndyzgy bet maj
night cream	түнкү бет май	tynky bet maj
day (as adj)	күндүзгү	kyndyzgy
night (as adj)	түнкү	tynky
tampon	тампон	tampon
toilet paper (toilet roll)	даарат кагазы	daarat kagazı
hair dryer	фен	fen

39. Jewelry

jewelry, jewels	зер буюмдар	zer bujumdar
precious (e.g., ~ stone)	баалуу	baaluu
hallmark stamp	проба	proba
ring	шакек	ʃakek
wedding ring	нике шакеги	nike ʃakegi
bracelet	билерик	bilerik
earrings	сөйкө	søjkø
necklace (~ of pearls)	шуру	ʃuru
crown	таажы	taadʒı
bead necklace	мончок	monʧok
diamond	бриллиант	brilliant
emerald	зымырыт	zımırıt
ruby	лаал	laal
sapphire	сапфир	sapfir
pearl	бермет	bermet
amber	янтарь	jantarʲ

40. Watches. Clocks

watch (wristwatch)	кол саат	kol saat
dial	циферблат	tsıferblat
hand (of clock, watch)	жебе	dʒebe
metal watch band	браслет	braslet
watch strap	кайыш кур	kajıʃ kur
battery	батарейка	batarejka

to be dead (battery)	зарядканын түгөнүүсү	zaŕadkanın tygønyysy
to change a battery	батарейка алмаштыруу	batarejka almaʃtıruu
to run fast	алдыга кетүү	aldıga ketyy
to run slow	калуу	kaluu
wall clock	дубалга тагуучу саат	dubalga taguutʃu saat
hourglass	кум саат	kum saat
sundial	күн саат	kyn saat
alarm clock	ойготкуч саат	ojgotkutʃ saat
watchmaker	саат устасы	saat ustası
to repair (vt)	оңдоо	oŋdoo

Food. Nutrición

41. Food

meat	эт	et
chicken	тоок	took
Rock Cornish hen (poussin)	балапан	balapan
duck	өрдөк	ørdøk
goose	каз	kaz
game	илбээсин	ilbeesin
turkey	күрп	kyrp
pork	чочко эти	tʃotʃko eti
veal	торпок эти	torpok eti
lamb	кой эти	koj eti
beef	уй эти	uj eti
rabbit	коен	koen
sausage (bologna, etc.)	колбаса	kolbasa
vienna sausage (frankfurter)	сосиска	sosiska
bacon	бекон	bekon
ham	ветчина	vettʃina
gammon	сан эт	san et
pâté	паштет	paʃtet
liver	боор	boor
hamburger (ground beef)	фарш	farʃ
tongue	тил	til
egg	жумуртка	dʒumurtka
eggs	жумурткалар	dʒumurtkalar
egg white	жумуртканын агы	dʒumurtkanın agı
egg yolk	жумуртканын сарысы	dʒumurtkanın sarısı
fish	балык	balık
seafood	деңиз азыктары	deɲiz azıktarı
crustaceans	рак сыяктуулар	rak sıjaktuular
caviar	урук	uruk
crab	краб	krab
shrimp	креветка	krevetka
oyster	устрица	ustritsa
spiny lobster	лангуст	langust
octopus	сегиз бут	segiz but

squid	капьмар	kalʲmar
sturgeon	осетрина	osetrina
salmon	лосось	lososʲ
halibut	палтус	paltus

cod	треска	treska
mackerel	скумбрия	skumbrija
tuna	тунец	tunets
eel	угорь	ugorʲ

trout	форель	forelʲ
sardine	сардина	sardina
pike	чортон	ʧorton
herring	сельдь	selʲdʲ

| bread | нан | nan |
| cheese | сыр | sır |

| sugar | кум шекер | kum-ʃeker |
| salt | туз | tuz |

rice	күрүч	kyryʧ
pasta (macaroni)	макарон	makaron
noodles	кесме	kesme

| butter | ак май | ak maj |
| vegetable oil | өсүмдүк майы | øsymdyk majı |

| sunflower oil | күн карама майы | kyn karama majı |
| margarine | маргарин | margarin |

| olives | зайтун | zajtun |
| olive oil | зайтун майы | zajtun majı |

milk	сүт	syt
condensed milk	коютулган сүт	kojɨtulgan syt
yogurt	йогурт	jogurt

| sour cream | сметана | smetana |
| cream (of milk) | каймак | kajmak |

| mayonnaise | майонез | majonez |
| buttercream | крем | krem |

groats (barley ~, etc.)	акшак	akʃak
flour	ун	un
canned food	консерва	konserva

cornflakes	жарылган жүгөрү	ʤarılgan ʤygøry
honey	бал	bal
jam	джем, конфитюр	ʤem, konfitɨr
chewing gum	сагыз	sagız

42. Drinks

water	суу	suu
drinking water	ичүүчү суу	iʧyyʧy suu
mineral water	минерал суусу	mineral suusu

still (adj)	газсыз	gazsız
carbonated (adj)	газдалган	gazdalgan
sparkling (adj)	газы менен	gazı menen
ice	муз	muz
with ice	музу менен	muzu menen

non-alcoholic (adj)	алкоголсуз	alkogolsuz
soft drink	алкоголсуз ичимдик	alkogolsuz iʧimdik
refreshing drink	суусундук	suusunduk
lemonade	лимонад	limonad

liquors	спирт ичимдиктери	spirt iʧimdikteri
wine	шарап	ʃarap
white wine	ак шарап	ak ʃarap
red wine	кызыл шарап	kızıl ʃarap

liqueur	ликёр	likʲor
champagne	шампан	ʃampan
vermouth	вермут	vermut

whiskey	виски	viski
vodka	арак	arak
gin	джин	dʒin
cognac	коньяк	konjak
rum	ром	rom

coffee	кофе	kofe
black coffee	кара кофе	kara kofe
coffee with milk	сүттөлгөн кофе	syttølgøn kofe
cappuccino	капучино	kapuʧino
instant coffee	эрүүчү кофе	eryyʧy kofe

milk	сүт	syt
cocktail	коктейль	koktejlʲ
milkshake	сүт коктейли	syt koktejli

juice	шире	ʃire
tomato juice	томат ширеси	tomat ʃiresi
orange juice	апельсин ширеси	apelʲsin ʃiresi
freshly squeezed juice	түз сыгылып алынган шире	tyz sıgılıp alıngan ʃire

beer	сыра	sıra
light beer	ачык сыра	aʧık sıra
dark beer	коңур сыра	koŋur sıra

tea	чай	tʃaj
black tea	кара чай	kara tʃaj
green tea	жашыл чай	dʒaʃɪl tʃaj

43. Vegetables

| vegetables | жашылча | dʒaʃɪltʃa |
| greens | көк чөп | køk tʃøp |

tomato	помидор	pomidor
cucumber	бадыраң	badıraŋ
carrot	сабиз	sabiz
potato	картошка	kartoʃka
onion	пияз	pijaz
garlic	сарымсак	sarımsak

cabbage	капуста	kapusta
cauliflower	гүлдүү капуста	gyldyy kapusta
Brussels sprouts	брюссель капустасы	brʉsselʲ kapustası
broccoli	брокколи капустасы	brokkoli kapustası

beet	кызылча	kızıltʃa
eggplant	баклажан	bakladʒan
zucchini	кабачок	kabatʃok
pumpkin	ашкабак	aʃkabak
turnip	шалгам	ʃalgam

parsley	петрушка	petruʃka
dill	укроп	ukrop
lettuce	салат	salat
celery	сельдерей	selʲderej
asparagus	спаржа	spardʒa
spinach	шпинат	ʃpinat

pea	нокот	nokot
beans	буурчак	buurtʃak
corn (maize)	жүгөрү	dʒygøry
kidney bean	төө буурчак	tøø buurtʃak

bell pepper	таттуу перец	tattuu perets
radish	шалгам	ʃalgam
artichoke	артишок	artiʃok

44. Fruits. Nuts

fruit	мөмө	mømø
apple	алма	alma
pear	алмурут	almurut

lemon	лимон	limon
orange	апельсин	apel'sin
strawberry (garden ~)	кулпунай	kulpunaj

mandarin	мандарин	mandarin
plum	кара өрүк	kara øryk
peach	шабдаалы	ʃabdaalı
apricot	өрүк	øryk
raspberry	дан куурай	dan kuuraj
pineapple	ананас	ananas

banana	банан	banan
watermelon	арбуз	arbuz
grape	жүзүм	dʒyzym
sour cherry	алча	alʧa
sweet cherry	гилас	gilas
melon	коон	koon

grapefruit	грейпфрут	grejpfrut
avocado	авокадо	avokado
papaya	папайя	papaja
mango	манго	mango
pomegranate	анар	anar

redcurrant	кызыл карагат	kızıl karagat
blackcurrant	кара карагат	kara karagat
gooseberry	крыжовник	krıdʒovnik
bilberry	кара моюл	kara mojʉl
blackberry	кара бүлдүркөн	kara byldyrkøn

raisin	мейиз	mejiz
fig	анжир	andʒir
date	курма	kurma

peanut	арахис	araχis
almond	бадам	badam
walnut	жаңгак	dʒaŋgak
hazelnut	токой жаңгагы	tokoj dʒaŋgagı
coconut	кокос жаңгагы	kokos dʒaŋgagı
pistachios	мисте	miste

45. Bread. Candy

bakers' confectionery (pastry)	кондитер азыктары	konditer azıktarı
bread	нан	nan
cookies	печенье	petʃenje

chocolate (n)	шоколад	ʃokolad
chocolate (as adj)	шоколаддан	ʃokoladdan

candy (wrapped)	конфета	konfeta
cake (e.g., cupcake)	пирожное	pirodʒnoe
cake (e.g., birthday ~)	торт	tort

| pie (e.g., apple ~) | пирог | pirog |
| filling (for cake, pie) | начинка | natʃinka |

jam (whole fruit jam)	кыям	kıjam
marmalade	мармелад	marmelad
wafers	вафли	vafli
ice-cream	бал муздак	bal muzdak
pudding	пудинг	puding

46. Cooked dishes

course, dish	тамак	tamak
cuisine	даам	daam
recipe	тамак жасоо ыкмасы	tamak dʒasoo ıkması
portion	порция	portsija

| salad | салат | salat |
| soup | сорпо | sorpo |

clear soup (broth)	ынак сорпо	ınak sorpo
sandwich (bread)	бутерброд	buterbrod
fried eggs	куурулган жумуртка	kuurulgan dʒumurtka

| hamburger (beefburger) | гамбургер | gamburger |
| beefsteak | бифштекс | bifʃteks |

side dish	гарнир	garnir
spaghetti	спагетти	spagetti
mashed potatoes	эзилген картошка	ezilgen kartoʃka
pizza	пицца	pitsa
porridge (oatmeal, etc.)	ботко	botko
omelet	омлет	omlet

boiled (e.g., ~ beef)	сууга бышырылган	suuga bıʃırılgan
smoked (adj)	ышталган	ıʃtalgan
fried (adj)	куурулган	kuurulgan
dried (adj)	кургатылган	kurgatılgan
frozen (adj)	тоңдурулган	toŋdurulgan
pickled (adj)	маринаддагы	marinaddagı

sweet (sugary)	таттуу	tattuu
salty (adj)	туздуу	tuzduu
cold (adj)	муздак	muzdak
hot (adj)	ысык	ısık
bitter (adj)	ачуу	atʃuu
tasty (adj)	даамдуу	daamduu

to cook in boiling water	кайнатуу	kajnatuu
to cook (dinner)	тамак бышыруу	tamak bıʃıruu
to fry (vt)	кууруу	kuuruu
to heat up (food)	жылытуу	dʒılıtuu

to salt (vt)	туздоо	tuzdoo
to pepper (vt)	калемпир кошуу	kalempir koʃuu
to grate (vt)	сүргүлөө	syrgyløø
peel (n)	сырты	sırtı
to peel (vt)	тазалоо	tazaloo

47. Spices

salt	туз	tuz
salty (adj)	туздуу	tuzduu
to salt (vt)	туздоо	tuzdoo

black pepper	кара мурч	kara murtʃ
red pepper (milled ~)	кызыл калемпир	kızıl kalempir
mustard	горчица	gortʃitsa
horseradish	хрен	χren

condiment	татымал	tatımal
spice	татымал	tatımal
sauce	соус	sous
vinegar	уксус	uksus

anise	анис	anis
basil	райхон	rajχon
cloves	гвоздика	gvozdika
ginger	имбирь	imbirⁱ
coriander	кориандр	koriandr
cinnamon	корица	koritsa

sesame	кунжут	kundʒut
bay leaf	лавр жалбырагы	lavr dʒalbıragı
paprika	паприка	paprika
caraway	зира	zira
saffron	заапаран	zaaparan

48. Meals

food	тамак	tamak
to eat (vi, vt)	тамактануу	tamaktanuu

breakfast	таңкы тамак	taŋkı tamak
to have breakfast	эртең менен тамактануу	erteŋ menen tamaktanuu

lunch	түшкү тамак	tүʃkү tamak
to have lunch	түштөнүү	tүʃtønyy
dinner	кечки тамак	ketʃki tamak
to have dinner	кечки тамакты ичүү	ketʃki tamaktı itʃyy

| appetite | табит | tabit |
| Enjoy your meal! | Тамагыңыз таттуу болсун! | tamagıŋız tattuu bolsun! |

to open (~ a bottle)	ачуу	atʃuu
to spill (liquid)	төгүп алуу	tøgyp aluu
to spill out (vi)	төгүлүү	tøgylyy

to boil (vi)	кайноо	kajnoo
to boil (vt)	кайнатуу	kajnatuu
boiled (~ water)	кайнатылган	kajnatılgan
to chill, cool down (vt)	суутуу	suutuu
to chill (vi)	сууп туруу	suup turuu

| taste, flavor | даам | daam |
| aftertaste | даамдануу | daamdanuu |

to slim down (lose weight)	арыктоо	arıktoo
diet	мүнөз тамак	mynøz tamak
vitamin	витамин	vitamin
calorie	калория	kalorija
vegetarian (n)	эттен чанган	etten tʃangan
vegetarian (adj)	этсиз даярдалган	etsiz dajardalgan

fats (nutrient)	майлар	majlar
proteins	белоктор	beloktor
carbohydrates	көмүрсуулар	kømyrsuular

slice (of lemon, ham)	кесим	kesim
piece (of cake, pie)	бөлүк	bølyk
crumb (of bread, cake, etc.)	күкүм	kykym

49. Table setting

spoon	кашык	kaʃık
knife	бычак	bıtʃak
fork	вилка	vilka

| cup (e.g., coffee ~) | чейчек | tʃøjtʃøk |
| plate (dinner ~) | табак | tabak |

saucer	табак	tabak
napkin (on table)	майлык	majlık
toothpick	тиш чукугуч	tiʃ tʃukugutʃ

50. Restaurant

restaurant	ресторан	restoran
coffee house	кофекана	kofekana
pub, bar	бар	bar
tearoom	чай салону	tʃaj salonu
waiter	официант	ofitsiant
waitress	официант кыз	ofitsiant kız
bartender	бармен	barmen
menu	меню	menü
wine list	шарап картасы	ʃarap kartası
to book a table	столду камдык	stoldu kamdık
	буйрутмалоо	bujrutmaloo
course, dish	тамак	tamak
to order (meal)	буйрутма кылуу	bujrutma kıluu
to make an order	буйрутма берүү	bujrutma beryy
aperitif	аперитив	aperitiv
appetizer	ысылык	ısılık
dessert	десерт	desert
check	эсеп	esep
to pay the check	эсеп төлөө	esep tøløø
to give change	майда акчаны кайтаруу	majda aktʃanı kajtaruu
tip	чайпул	tʃajpul

Family, relatives and friends

51. Personal information. Forms

name (first name)	аты	atı
surname (last name)	фамилиясы	familijası
date of birth	төрөлгөн күнү	tørølgøn kyny
place of birth	туулган жери	tuulgan dʒeri
nationality	улуту	ulutu
place of residence	жашаган жери	dʒaʃagan dʒeri
country	өлкө	ølkø
profession (occupation)	кесиби	kesibi
gender, sex	жынысы	dʒınısı
height	бою	bojʉ
weight	салмак	salmak

52. Family members. Relatives

mother	эне	ene
father	ата	ata
son	уул	uul
daughter	кыз	kız
younger daughter	кичүү кыз	kitʃyy kız
younger son	кичүү уул	kitʃyy uul
eldest daughter	улуу кыз	uluu kız
eldest son	улуу уул	uluu uul
brother	бир тууган	bir tuugan
elder brother	байке	bajke
younger brother	ини	ini
sister	бир тууган	bir tuugan
elder sister	эже	edʒe
younger sister	синди	siŋdi
cousin (masc.)	атасы же энеси бир тууган	atası dʒe enesi bir tuugan
cousin (fem.)	атасы же энеси бир тууган	atası dʒe enesi bir tuugan
mom, mommy	апа	apa
dad, daddy	ата	ata

parents	ата-эне	ata-ene
child	бала	bala
children	балдар	baldar

grandmother	чоң апа	tʃoŋ apa
grandfather	чоң ата	tʃoŋ ata
grandson	небере бала	nebere bala
granddaughter	небере кыз	nebere kız
grandchildren	неберелер	nebereler

uncle	таяке	tajake
aunt	таяже	tajadʒe
nephew	ини	ini
niece	жээн	dʒeen

mother-in-law (wife's mother)	кайын эне	kajın ene
father-in-law (husband's father)	кайын ата	kajın ata
son-in-law (daughter's husband)	күйөө бала	kyjøø bala
stepmother	өгөй эне	øgøj ene
stepfather	өгөй ата	øgøj ata

infant	эмчектеги бала	emtʃektegi bala
baby (infant)	ымыркай	ımırkaj
little boy, kid	бөбөк	bøbøk

wife	аял	ajal
husband	эр	er
spouse (husband)	күйөө	kyjøø
spouse (wife)	зайып	zajıp

married (masc.)	аялы бар	ajalı bar
married (fem.)	күйөөдө	kyjøødø
single (unmarried)	бойдок	bojdok
bachelor	бойдок	bojdok
divorced (masc.)	ажырашкан	adʒıraʃkan
widow	жесир	dʒesir
widower	жесир	dʒesir

relative	тууган	tuugan
close relative	жакын тууган	dʒakın tuugan
distant relative	алыс тууган	alıs tuugan
relatives	бир тууган	bir tuugan

orphan (boy or girl)	жетим	dʒetim
guardian (of a minor)	камкорчу	kamkortʃu
to adopt (a boy)	уул кылып асырап алуу	uul kılıp asırap aluu
to adopt (a girl)	кыз кылып асырап алуу	kız kılıp asırap aluu

53. Friends. Coworkers

friend (masc.)	дос	dos
friend (fem.)	курбу	kurbu
friendship	достук	dostuk
to be friends	достошуу	dostoʃuu
buddy (masc.)	шерик	ʃerik
buddy (fem.)	шерик кыз	ʃerik kız
partner	өнөктөш	ønøktøʃ
chief (boss)	башчы	baʃtʃı
superior (n)	башчы	baʃtʃı
owner, proprietor	кожоюн	kodʒodʒʉn
subordinate (n)	кол астындагы	kol astındagı
colleague	кесиптеш	kesipteʃ
acquaintance (person)	тааныш	taanıʃ
fellow traveler	жолдош	dʒoldoʃ
classmate	классташ	klasstaʃ
neighbor (masc.)	кошуна	koʃuna
neighbor (fem.)	кошуна	koʃuna
neighbors	кошуналар	koʃunalar

54. Man. Woman

woman	аял	ajal
girl (young woman)	кыз	kız
bride	колукту	koluktu
beautiful (adj)	сулуу	suluu
tall (adj)	бою узун	bojʉ uzun
slender (adj)	сымбаттуу	sımbattuu
short (adj)	орто бойлуу	orto bojluu
blonde (n)	ак саргыл чачтуу	ak sargıl tʃatʃtuu
brunette (n)	кара чачтуу	kara tʃatʃtuu
ladies' (adj)	аялдардын	ajaldardın
virgin (girl)	эркек көрө элек кыз	erkek kørø elek kız
pregnant (adj)	кош бойлуу	koʃ bojluu
man (adult male)	эркек	erkek
blond (n)	ак саргыл чачтуу	ak sargıl tʃatʃtuu
brunet (n)	кара чачтуу	kara tʃatʃtuu
tall (adj)	бийик бойлуу	bijik bojluu
short (adj)	орто бойлуу	orto bojluu
rude (rough)	орой	oroj

stocky (adj)	жапалдаш бой	ʤapaldaʃ boj
robust (adj)	чымыр	ʧɪmɪr
strong (adj)	күчтүү	kyʧtyy
strength	күч	kyʧ

stout, fat (adj)	толук	toluk
swarthy (adj)	кара тору	kara toru
slender (well-built)	сымбаттуу	sɪmbattuu
elegant (adj)	жарашып кийинген	ʤaraʃɪp kijingen

55. Age

age	жаш	ʤaʃ
youth (young age)	жаштык	ʤaʃtɪk
young (adj)	жаш	ʤaʃ

younger (adj)	кичүү	kiʧyy
older (adj)	улуу	uluu

young man	улан	ulan
teenager	өспүрүм	øspyrym
guy, fellow	жигит	ʤigit

old man	абышка	abɪʃka
old woman	кемпир	kempir

adult (adj)	чоң киши	ʧoŋ kiʃi
middle-aged (adj)	орто жаш	orto ʤaʃ
elderly (adj)	жашап калган	ʤaʃap kalgan
old (adj)	картаң	kartaŋ

retirement	бааракы	baarakɪ
to retire (from job)	ардактуу эс алууга чыгуу	ardaktuu es aluuga ʧɪguu
retiree	бааргер	baarger

56. Children

child	бала	bala
children	балдар	baldar
twins	эгиздер	egizder

cradle	бешик	beʃik
rattle	шырылдак	ʃɪrɪldak
diaper	жалаяк	ʤalajak

pacifier	упчу	upʧu
baby carriage	бешик араба	beʃik araba

kindergarten	бала бакча	bala bakʧa
babysitter	бала баккыч	bala bakkıʧ
childhood	балалык	balalık
doll	куурчак	kuurʧak
toy	оюнчук	ojʉnʧuk
construction set (toy)	конструктор	konstruktor
well-bred (adj)	тарбия көргөн	tarbija kørgøn
ill-bred (adj)	жетесиз	dʒetesiz
spoiled (adj)	эрке	erke
to be naughty	тентектик кылуу	tentektik kıluu
mischievous (adj)	тентек	tentek
mischievousness	шоктук, тентектик	ʃoktuk, tentektik
mischievous child	тентек	tentek
obedient (adj)	элпек	elpek
disobedient (adj)	тил албас	til albas
docile (adj)	зээндүү	zeendyy
clever (smart)	акылдуу	akılduu
child prodigy	вундеркинд	vunderkind

57. Married couples. Family life

to kiss (vt)	өбүү	øbyy
to kiss (vi)	өбүшүү	øbyʃyy
family (n)	үй-бүлө	yj-bylø
family (as adj)	үй-бүлөлүү	yj-bylølyy
couple	эрди-катын	erdi-katın
marriage (state)	нике	nike
hearth (home)	үй очогу	yj oʧogu
dynasty	династия	dinastija
date	жолугушуу	dʒoluguʃuu
kiss	өбүү	øbyy
love (for sb)	сүйүү	syjyy
to love (sb)	сүйүү	syjyy
beloved	жакшы көргөн	dʒakʃı kørgøn
tenderness	назиктик	naziktik
tender (affectionate)	назик	nazik
faithfulness	берилгендик	berilgendik
faithful (adj)	ишенимдүү	iʃenimdyy
care (attention)	кам көрүү	kam køryy
caring (~ father)	камкор	kamkor
newlyweds	жаңы үйлөнүшкөндөр	dʒaŋı yjlønyʃkøndør
honeymoon	таттуулашуу	tattuulaʃuu

to get married (ab. woman)	күйөөгө чыгуу	kyjøøgø ʧɪguu
to get married (ab. man)	аял алуу	ajal aluu
wedding	үйлөнүү той	yilønyy toɣ
golden wedding	алтын үлпөт той	altɪn ylpøt toj
anniversary	жылдык	dʒɪldɪk
lover (masc.)	ойнош	ojnoʃ
mistress (lover)	ойнош	ojnoʃ
adultery	көзгө чөп салуу	køzgø ʧøp saluu
to cheat on ... (commit adultery)	көзгө чөп салуу	køzgø ʧøp saluu
jealous (adj)	кызгануу	kɪzganuu
to be jealous	кызгануу	kɪzganuu
divorce	ажырашуу	adʒɪraʃuu
to divorce (vi)	ажырашуу	adʒɪraʃuu
to quarrel (vi)	урушуу	uruʃuu
to be reconciled (after an argument)	жарашуу	dʒaraʃuu
together (adv)	бирге	birge
sex	жыныстык катнаш	dʒɪnɪstɪk katnaʃ
happiness	бакыт	bakɪt
happy (adj)	бактылуу	baktɪluu
misfortune (accident)	кырсык	kɪrsɪk
unhappy (adj)	бактысыз	baktɪsɪz

Character. Feelings. Emotions

58. Feelings. Emotions

feeling (emotion)	сезим	sezim
feelings	сезим	sezim
to feel (vt)	сезүү	sezyy
hunger	ачка болуу	atʃka boluu
to be hungry	ачка болуу	atʃka boluu
thirst	чаңкоо	tʃaŋkoo
to be thirsty	суусап калуу	suusap kaluu
sleepiness	уйкусу келүү	ujkusu kelyy
to feel sleepy	уйкусу келүү	ujkusu kelyy
tiredness	чарчоо	tʃartʃoo
tired (adj)	чарчаңкы	tʃartʃaŋkı
to get tired	чарчоо	tʃartʃoo
mood (humor)	көңүл	køŋyl
boredom	зеригүү	zerigyy
to be bored	зеригүү	zerigyy
seclusion	элден качуу	elden katʃuu
to seclude oneself	элден качуу	elden katʃuu
to worry (make anxious)	көңүлүн бөлүү	køŋylyn bølyy
to be worried	сарсанаа болуу	sarsanaa boluu
worrying (n)	кабатырлануу	kabatırlanuu
anxiety	чочулоо	tʃotʃuloo
preoccupied (adj)	бушайман	buʃajman
to be nervous	тынчы кетүү	tıntʃı ketyy
to panic (vi)	дүрбөлөңгө түшүү	dyrbøløŋgø tyʃyy
hope	үмүт	ymyt
to hope (vi, vt)	үмүттөнүү	ymyttønyy
certainty	ишенимдүүлүк	iʃenimdyylyk
certain, sure (adj)	ишеничтүү	iʃenitʃtyy
uncertainty	ишенбегендик	iʃenbegendik
uncertain (adj)	ишенбеген	iʃenbegen
drunk (adj)	мас	mas
sober (adj)	соо	soo
weak (adj)	бошоң	boʃoŋ
happy (adj)	бактылуу	baktıluu
to scare (vt)	жүрөгүн түшүрүү	dʒyrøgyn tyʃyryy

| fury (madness) | жинденүү | dʒindenyy |
| rage (fury) | жаалдануу | dʒaaldanuu |

depression	көңүлү чөгүү	køŋyly tʃøgyy
discomfort (unease)	ыңгайсыз	ıŋgajsız
comfort	ыңгайлуу	ıŋgajluu
to regret (be sorry)	өкүнүү	økynyy
regret	өкүнүп калуу	økynyp kaluu
bad luck	жолу болбоо	dʒolu bolboo
sadness	капалануу	kapalanuu

shame (remorse)	уят	ujat
gladness	кубаныч	kubanıtʃ
enthusiasm, zeal	ынта менен	ınta menen
enthusiast	ынтызар	ıntızar
to show enthusiasm	ынтасын көрсөтүү	ıntasın kørsøtyy

59. Character. Personality

character	мүнөз	mynøz
character flaw	кемчилик	kemtʃilik
mind	эс-акыл	es-akıl
reason	акыл	akıl

conscience	абийир	abijir
habit (custom)	адат	adat
ability (talent)	жөндөм	dʒøndøm
can (e.g., ~ swim)	билүү	bilyy

patient (adj)	көтөрүмдүү	køtørymdyy
impatient (adj)	чыдамы жок	tʃıdamı dʒok
curious (inquisitive)	ынтызар	ıntızar
curiosity	кызыгуучулук	kızıguutʃuluk

modesty	жөнөкөйлүк	dʒønøkøjlyk
modest (adj)	жөнөкөй	dʒønøkøj
immodest (adj)	чекилик	tʃekilik

laziness	жалкоолук	dʒalkooluk
lazy (adj)	жалкоо	dʒalkoo
lazy person (masc.)	эринчээк	erintʃeek

cunning (n)	куулук	kuuluk
cunning (as adj)	куу	kuu
distrust	ишенбөөчүлүк	iʃenbøøtʃylyk
distrustful (adj)	ишенбеген	iʃenbegen

generosity	берешендик	bereʃendik
generous (adj)	берешен	bereʃen
talented (adj)	зээндүү	zeendyy

talent	талант	talant
courageous (adj)	кайраттуу	kajrattuu
courage	кайрат	kajrat
honest (adj)	чынчыл	tʃintʃɪl
honesty	чынчылдык	tʃintʃɪldɪk

careful (cautious)	сак	sak
brave (courageous)	тайманбас	tajmanbas
serious (adj)	оор басырыктуу	oor basɪrɪktuu
strict (severe, stern)	сүрдүү	syrdyy

decisive (adj)	чечкиндүү	tʃetʃkindyy
indecisive (adj)	чечкинсиз	tʃetʃkinsiz
shy, timid (adj)	тартынчаак	tartɪntʃaak
shyness, timidity	жүрөкзаада	dʒyrøkzaada

confidence (trust)	ишеним артуу	iʃenim artuu
to believe (trust)	ишенүү	iʃenyy
trusting (credulous)	ишенчээк	iʃentʃeek

sincerely (adv)	чын жүрөктөн	tʃɪn dʒyrøktøn
sincere (adj)	ак ниеттен	ak nietten
sincerity	ак ниеттүүлүк	ak niettyylyk
open (person)	ачык	atʃɪk

calm (adj)	жоош	dʒooʃ
frank (sincere)	ачык	atʃɪk
naïve (adj)	ишенчээк	iʃentʃeek
absent-minded (adj)	унутчаак	unuttʃaak
funny (odd)	кызык	kɪzɪk

greed, stinginess	ач көздүк	atʃ køzdyk
greedy, stingy (adj)	сараң	saraŋ
stingy (adj)	сараң	saraŋ
evil (adj)	каардуу	kaarduu
stubborn (adj)	көк	køk
unpleasant (adj)	жагымсыз	dʒagɪmsɪz

selfish person (masc.)	өзүмчүл	øzymtʃyl
selfish (adj)	өзүмчүл	øzymtʃyl
coward	суу жүрөк	suu dʒyrøk
cowardly (adj)	суу жүрөк	suu dʒyrøk

60. Sleep. Dreams

to sleep (vi)	уктоо	uktoo
sleep, sleeping	уйку	ujku
dream	түш	tyʃ
to dream (in sleep)	түш көрүү	tyʃ køryy
sleepy (adj)	уйкусураган	ujkusuragan

bed	керебет	kerebet
mattress	матрас	matras
blanket (comforter)	жууркан	dʒuurkan
pillow	жаздык	dʒazdık
sheet	шейшеп	ʃeiʃep

insomnia	уйкусуздук	ujkusuzduk
sleepless (adj)	уйкусуз	ujkusuz
sleeping pill	уйку дарысы	ujku darısı
to take a sleeping pill	уйку дарысын ичүү	ujku darısın itʃyy

to feel sleepy	уйкусу келүү	ujkusu kelyy
to yawn (vi)	эстөө	estøø
to go to bed	уктоого кетүү	uktoogo ketyy
to make up the bed	төшөк салуу	tøʃøk saluu
to fall asleep	уктап калуу	uktap kaluu

nightmare	коркунучтуу түш	korkunutʃtuu tyʃ
snore, snoring	коңурук	koŋuruk
to snore (vi)	коңурук тартуу	koŋuruk tartuu

alarm clock	ойготкуч саат	ojgotkutʃ saat
to wake (vt)	ойготуу	ojgotuu
to wake up	ойгонуу	ojgonuu
to get up (vi)	төшөктөн туруу	tøʃøktøn turuu
to wash up (wash face)	бети-колду жуу	beti-koldu dʒuu

61. Humour. Laughter. Gladness

humor (wit, fun)	күлкү салуу	kylky saluu
sense of humor	тамашага чалуу	tamaʃaga tʃaluu
to enjoy oneself	көңүл ачуу	køŋyl atʃuu
cheerful (merry)	көңүлдүү	køŋyldyy
merriment (gaiety)	көңүлдүүлүк	køŋyldyylyk

smile	жылмайыш	dʒılmajıʃ
to smile (vi)	жылмаюу	dʒılmadʒuu
to start laughing	күлүп жиберүү	kylyp dʒiberyy
to laugh (vi)	күлүү	kylyy
laugh, laughter	күлкү	kylky

anecdote	күлкүлүү окуя	kylkylyy okuja
funny (anecdote, etc.)	күлкүлүү	kylkylyy
funny (odd)	кызык	kızık

to joke (vi)	тамашалоо	tamaʃaloo
joke (verbal)	тамаша	tamaʃa
joy (emotion)	кубаныч	kubanıtʃ
to rejoice (vi)	кубануу	kubanuu
joyful (adj)	кубанычтуу	kubanıtʃtuu

62. Discussion, conversation. Part 1

communication	баарлашуу	baarlaʃuu
to communicate	баарлашуу	baarlaʃuu
conversation	сүйлөшүү	syjløʃyy
dialog	маек	maek
discussion (discourse)	талкуу	talkuu
dispute (debate)	талаш	talaʃ
to dispute	талашуу	talaʃuu
interlocutor	аңгемелешкен	aŋgemeleʃken
topic (theme)	тема	tema
point of view	көз караш	køz karaʃ
opinion (point of view)	ой-пикир	oj-pikir
speech (talk)	сөз	søz
discussion (of report, etc.)	талкуу	talkuu
to discuss (vt)	талкуулоо	talkuuloo
talk (conversation)	маек	maek
to talk (to chat)	маектешүү	maekteʃyy
meeting (encounter)	жолугушуу	dʒoluguʃuu
to meet (vi, vt)	жолугушуу	dʒoluguʃuu
proverb	макал-лакап	makal-lakap
saying	лакап	lakap
riddle (poser)	табышмак	tabıʃmak
to pose a riddle	табышмак айтуу	tabıʃmak ajtuu
password	сырсөз	sırsøz
secret	сыр	sır
oath (vow)	ант	ant
to swear (an oath)	ант берүү	ant beryy
promise	убада	ubada
to promise (vt)	убада берүү	ubada beryy
advice (counsel)	кеңеш	keŋeʃ
to advise (vt)	кеңеш берүү	keŋeʃ beryy
to follow one's advice	кеңешин жолдоо	keŋeʃin dʒoldoo
to listen to … (obey)	угуу	uguu
news	жаңылык	dʒaŋılık
sensation (news)	дүң салуу	dyŋ saluu
information (report)	маалымат	maalımat
conclusion (decision)	корутунду	korutundu
voice	үн	yn
compliment	мактоо	maktoo
kind (nice)	сылык	sılık
word	сөз	søz
phrase	сүйлөм	syjløm

answer	жооп	dʒoop
truth	чындык	tʃındık
lie	жалган	dʒalgan

thought	ой	oj
idea (inspiration)	ой	oj
fantasy	ойдон чыгаруу	ojdon tʃıgaruu

63. Discussion, conversation. Part 2

respected (adj)	урматтуу	urmattuu
to respect (vt)	сыйлоо	sıjloo
respect	урмат	urmat
Dear ... (letter)	Урматтуу ...	urmattuu ...

to introduce (sb to sb)	тааныштыруу	taanıʃtıruu
to make acquaintance	таанышуу	taanıʃuu

intention	ниет	niet
to intend (have in mind)	ниеттенүү	niettenyy
wish	каалоо	kaaloo
to wish (~ good luck)	каалоо айтуу	kaaloo ajtuu

surprise (astonishment)	таңгалыч	taŋgalıtʃ
to surprise (amaze)	таң калтыруу	taŋ kaltıruu
to be surprised	таң калуу	taŋ kaluu

to give (vt)	берүү	beryy
to take (get hold of)	алуу	aluu
to give back	кайтарып берүү	kajtarıp beryy
to return (give back)	кайра берүү	kajra beryy

to apologize (vi)	кечирим суроо	ketʃirim suroo
apology	кечирим	ketʃirim
to forgive (vt)	кечирүү	ketʃiryy

to talk (speak)	сүйлөшүү	syjløʃyy
to listen (vi)	угуу	uguu
to hear out	кулак салуу	kulak saluu
to understand (vt)	түшүнүү	tyʃynyy

to show (to display)	көрсөтүү	kørsøtyy
to look at ...	... кароо	... karoo
to call (yell for sb)	чакыруу	tʃakıruu
to distract (disturb)	тынчын алуу	tıntʃın aluu
to disturb (vt)	тынчын алуу	tıntʃın aluu
to pass (to hand sth)	узатып коюу	uzatıp kojuu

demand (request)	сураныч	suranıtʃ
to request (ask)	суроо	suroo

| demand (firm request) | тапап | talap |
| to demand (request firmly) | талап кылуу | talap kıluu |

to tease (call names)	кыжырына тийүү	kıdʒırına tijyy
to mock (make fun of)	шылдыңдоо	ʃildıŋdoo
mockery, derision	шылдың	ʃildıŋ
nickname	лакап ат	lakap at

insinuation	кыйытма	kıjıtma
to insinuate (imply)	кыйытып айтуу	kıjıtıp aytuu
to mean (vt)	билдирүү	bildiryy

description	сүрөттөө	syrøttøø
to describe (vt)	сүрөттөп берүү	syrøttøp beryy
praise (compliments)	алкыш	alkıʃ
to praise (vt)	мактоо	maktoo

disappointment	көңүлү калуу	køŋyly kaluu
to disappoint (vt)	көңүлүн калтыруу	køŋylyn kaltıruu
to be disappointed	көңүл калуу	køŋyl kaluu

supposition	божомол	bodʒomol
to suppose (assume)	божомолдоо	bodʒomoldoo
warning (caution)	эскертүү	eskertyy
to warn (vt)	эскертүү	eskertyy

64. Discussion, conversation. Part 3

| to talk into (convince) | көндүрүү | køndyryy |
| to calm down (vt) | тынчтандыруу | tıntʃtandıruu |

silence (~ is golden)	жымжырт	dʒımdʒırt
to be silent (not speaking)	унчукпоо	untʃukpoo
to whisper (vi, vt)	шыбыроо	ʃibıroo
whisper	шыбыр	ʃibır

| frankly, sincerely (adv) | ачык айтканда | atʃık ajtkanda |
| in my opinion ... | менин оюмча ... | menin ojumtʃa ... |

detail (of the story)	ийне-жиби	ijne-dʒibi
detailed (adj)	тетиктелген	tetiktelgen
in detail (adv)	тетикке чейин	tetikke tʃejin

| hint, clue | четин чыгаруу | tʃetin tʃıgaruu |
| to give a hint | четин чыгаруу | tʃetin tʃıgaruu |

look (glance)	көз	køz
to have a look	карап коюу	karap kojuu
fixed (look)	тиктеген	tiktegen
to blink (vi)	көз ирмөө	køz irmøø

| to wink (vi) | көз кысуу | køz kısuu |
| to nod (in assent) | баш ийкөө | baʃ ijkøø |

sigh	дем чыгаруу	dem tʃigaruu
to sigh (vi)	дем алуу	dem aluu
to shudder (vi)	селт этүү	selt etyy
gesture	жаңсоо	dʒaŋsoo
to touch (one's arm, etc.)	тийип кетүү	tijip ketyy
to seize	кармоо	karmoo
(e.g., ~ by the arm)		
to tap (on the shoulder)	таптоо	taptoo

Look out!	Абайлагыла!	abajlagıla!
Really?	Чын элеби?!	tʃın elebi?!
Are you sure?	Жаңылган жоксуңбу?	dʒaŋılgan dʒoksuŋbu?
Good luck!	Ийгилик!	ijgilik!
I see!	Түшүнүктүү!	tyʃynyktyy!
What a pity!	Кап!	kap!

65. Agreement. Refusal

consent	макулдук	makulduk
to consent (vi)	макул болуу	makul boluu
approval	колдоо	koldoo
to approve (vt)	колдоо	koldoo
refusal	баш тартуу	baʃ tartuu
to refuse (vi, vt)	баш тартуу	baʃ tartuu

Great!	Эң жакшы!	eŋ dʒakʃı!
All right!	Жакшы!	dʒakʃı!
Okay! (I agree)	Макул!	makul!

forbidden (adj)	тыюу салынган	tıjuu salıngan
it's forbidden	болбойт	bolbojt
it's impossible	мүмкүн эмес	mymkyn emes
incorrect (adj)	туура эмес	tuura emes

to reject (~ a demand)	четке кагуу	tʃetke kaguu
to support (cause, idea)	колдоо	koldoo
to accept (~ an apology)	кабыл алуу	kabıl aluu

to confirm (vt)	ырастоо	ırastoo
confirmation	ырастоо	ırastoo
permission	уруксат	uruksat
to permit (vt)	уруксат берүү	uruksat beryy
decision	чечим	tʃetʃim
to say nothing	унчукпоо	untʃukpoo
(hold one's tongue)		
condition (term)	шарт	ʃart
excuse (pretext)	шылтоо	ʃıltoo

| praise (compliments) | алкыш | alkıʃ |
| to praise (vt) | мактоо | maktoo |

66. Success. Good luck. Failure

success	ийгилик	ijgilik
successfully (adv)	ийгиликтүү	ijgiliktyy
successful (adj)	ийгиликтүү	ijgiliktyy

luck (good luck)	жол болуу	dʒol boluu
Good luck!	Ийгилик!	ijgilik!
lucky (e.g., ~ day)	ийгиликтүү	ijgiliktyy
lucky (fortunate)	жолу бар	dʒolu bar

failure	жолу болбостук	dʒolu bolbostuk
misfortune	жолу болбостук	dʒolu bolbostuk
bad luck	жолу болбоо	dʒolu bolboo
unsuccessful (adj)	жолу болбогон	dʒolu bolbogon
catastrophe	киши көрбөсүн	kiʃi kørbøsyn

pride	сыймык	sıjmık
proud (adj)	көтөрүнгөн	køtøryngøn
to be proud	сыймыктануу	sıjmıktanuu

winner	жеңүүчү	dʒeŋyytʃy
to win (vi)	жеңүү	dʒeŋyy
to lose (not win)	жеңилүү	dʒeŋilyy
try	аракет	araket
to try (vi)	аракет кылуу	araket kıluu
chance (opportunity)	мүмкүнчүлүк	mymkyntʃylyk

67. Quarrels. Negative emotions

shout (scream)	кыйкырык	kıjkırık
to shout (vi)	кыйкыруу	kıjkıruu
to start to cry out	кыйкырып алуу	kıjkırıp aluu

quarrel	уруш	uruʃ
to quarrel (vi)	урушуу	uruʃuu
fight (squabble)	чатак	tʃatak
to make a scene	чататашуу	tʃataktaʃuu
conflict	чыр-чатак	tʃır-tʃatak
misunderstanding	түшүнбөстүк	tyʃynbøstyk

insult	кордоо	kordoo
to insult (vt)	кемсинтүү	kemsintyy
insulted (adj)	катуу тийген	katuu tijgen
resentment	таарыныч	taarınıtʃ

| to offend (vt) | көңүлгө тийүү | køŋylgø tijyy |
| to take offense | таарынып калуу | taarınıp kaluu |

indignation	нааразылык	naarazılık
to be indignant	нааразы болуу	naarazı boluu
complaint	арыз	arız
to complain (vi, vt)	арыздануу	arızdanuu

apology	кечирим	ketʃirim
to apologize (vi)	кечирим суроо	ketʃirim suroo
to beg pardon	кечирим суроо	ketʃirim suroo

criticism	сын-пикир	sın-pikir
to criticize (vt)	сындоо	sındoo
accusation (charge)	айыптоо	ajıptoo
to accuse (vt)	айыптоо	ajıptoo

| revenge | өч алуу | øtʃ aluu |
| to avenge (get revenge) | өч алуу | øtʃ aluu |

disdain	киши катары көрбөө	kiʃi katarı kørbøø
to despise (vt)	киши катарына албоо	kiʃi katarına alboo
hatred, hate	жек көрүү	dʒek køryy
to hate (vt)	жек көрүү	dʒek køryy

nervous (adj)	тынчы кеткен	tıntʃı ketken
to be nervous	тынчы кетүү	tıntʃı ketyy
angry (mad)	ачууланган	atʃuulangan
to make angry	ачуусун келтирүү	atʃuusun keltiryy

humiliation	кемсинтүү	kemsintyy
to humiliate (vt)	кемсинтүү	kemsintyy
to humiliate oneself	байкуш болуу	bajkuʃ boluu

| shock | дендирөө | dendirøø |
| to shock (vt) | дендиретүү | dendiretyy |

| trouble (e.g., serious ~) | жагымсыз жагдай | dʒagımsız dʒagdaj |
| unpleasant (adj) | жагымсыз | dʒagımsız |

fear (dread)	коркунуч	korkunutʃ
terrible (storm, heat)	каардуу	kaarduu
scary (e.g., ~ story)	коркунучтуу	korkunutʃtuu
horror	үрөй учуу	yrøj utʃuu
awful (crime, news)	үрөй учуруу	yrøj utʃuruu

to begin to tremble	калтырап баштоо	kaltırap baʃtoo
to cry (weep)	ыйлоо	ıjloo
to start crying	ыйлап жиберүү	ıjlap dʒiberyy
tear	көз жаш	køz dʒaʃ
fault	күнөө	kynøø
guilt (feeling)	күнөө сезими	kynøø sezimi

dishonor (disgrace)	уят	uјɑt
protest	нааразылык	naarazılık
stress	**бушайман болуу**	buʃajman boluu

to disturb (vt)	**тынчын алуу**	tıntʃın aluu
to be furious	**жини келүү**	dʒini kelyy
mad, angry (adj)	**ачуулуу**	atʃuuluu
to end (~ a relationship)	**токтотуу**	toktotuu
to swear (at sb)	**урушуу**	uruʃuu

to scare (become afraid)	**чоочуу**	tʃootʃuu
to hit (strike with hand)	**уруу**	uruu
to fight (street fight, etc.)	**мушташуу**	muʃtaʃuu

to settle (a conflict)	**жөндөө**	dʒøndøø
discontented (adj)	**нааразы**	naarazı
furious (adj)	**жаалданган**	dʒaaldangan

| It's not good! | **Бул жакшы эмес!** | bul dʒakʃı emes! |
| It's bad! | **Бул жаман!** | bul dʒaman! |

Medicine

68. Diseases

sickness	оору	ooru
to be sick	ооруу	ooruu
health	ден-соолук	den-sooluk
runny nose (coryza)	мурдунан суу агуу	murdunan suu aguu
tonsillitis	ангина	angina
cold (illness)	суук тийүү	suuk tijyy
to catch a cold	суук тийгизип алуу	suuk tijgizip aluu
bronchitis	бронхит	bronχit
pneumonia	кабыргадан сезгенүү	kabırgadan sezgenyy
flu, influenza	сасык тумоо	sasık tumoo
nearsighted (adj)	алыстан көрө албоо	alıstan kørø alboo
farsighted (adj)	жакындан көрө албоо	dʒakından kørø alboo
strabismus (crossed eyes)	кылый көздүүлүк	kılıj køzdyylyk
cross-eyed (adj)	кылый көздүүлүк	kılıj køzdyylyk
cataract	челкөз	tʃelkøz
glaucoma	глаукома	glaukoma
stroke	мээге кан куюлуу	meege kan kujʉluu
heart attack	инфаркт	infarkt
myocardial infarction	инфаркт миокарда	infarkt miokarda
paralysis	шал	ʃal
to paralyze (vt)	шал болуу	ʃal boluu
allergy	аллергия	allergija
asthma	астма	astma
diabetes	диабет	diabet
toothache	тиш оорусу	tiʃ oorusu
caries	кариес	karies
diarrhea	ич өткү	itʃ øtky
constipation	ич катуу	itʃ katuu
stomach upset	ич бузулгандык	itʃ buzulgandık
food poisoning	уулануу	uulanuu
to get food poisoning	уулануу	uulanuu
arthritis	артрит	artrit
rickets	итий	itij
rheumatism	кызыл жүгүрүк	kızıl dʒygyryk

atherosclerosis	атеросклероз	aterosкıderoz
gastritis	карын сезгенүүсу	karın sezgenyysu
appendicitis	аппендицит	appenditsit
cholecystitis	холецистит	χoletsistit
ulcer	жара	dʒara

measles	кызылча	kızıltʃa
rubella (German measles)	кызамык	kızamık
jaundice	сарык	sarık
hepatitis	гепатит	gepatit

schizophrenia	шизофрения	ʃizofrenija
rabies (hydrophobia)	кутурма	kuturma
neurosis	невроз	nevroz
concussion	мээнин чайкалышы	meenin tʃajkalıʃı

cancer	рак	rak
sclerosis	склероз	skleroz
multiple sclerosis	жайылган склероз	dʒajılgan skleroz

alcoholism	аракечтик	araketʃtik
alcoholic (n)	аракеч	araketʃ
syphilis	котон жара	koton dʒara
AIDS	СПИД	spid

tumor	шишик	ʃiʃik
malignant (adj)	залалдуу	zalalduu
benign (adj)	залалсыз	zalalsız

fever	безгек	bezgek
malaria	безгек	bezgek
gangrene	кабыз	kabız
seasickness	деңиз оорусу	deŋiz oorusu
epilepsy	талма	talma

epidemic	эпидемия	epidemija
typhus	келте	kelte
tuberculosis	кургак учук	kurgak utʃuk
cholera	холера	χolera
plague (bubonic ~)	кара тумоо	kara tumoo

69. Symptoms. Treatments. Part 1

symptom	белги	belgi
temperature	дене табынын көтөрүлүшү	dene tabının køtørylyʃy
high temperature (fever)	жогорку температура	dʒogorku temperatura
pulse (heartbeat)	тамыр кагышы	tamır kagıʃı
dizziness (vertigo)	баш айлануу	baʃ ajlanuu
hot (adj)	ысык	ısık

shivering	чыйрыгуу	ʧijrɪguu
pale (e.g., ~ face)	купкуу	kupkuu
cough	жөтөл	ʤɵtɵl
to cough (vi)	жөтөлүү	ʤɵtɵlyy
to sneeze (vi)	чүчкүрүү	ʧyʧkyryy
faint	эси оо	esi oo
to faint (vi)	эси ооп жыгылуу	esi oop ʤɪgɪluu
bruise (hématome)	көк-ала	kɵk-ala
bump (lump)	шишик	ʃiʃik
to bang (bump)	урунуп алуу	urunup aluu
contusion (bruise)	көгөртүп алуу	kɵgɵrtyp aluu
to get a bruise	көгөртүп алуу	kɵgɵrtyp aluu
to limp (vi)	аксоо	aksoo
dislocation	муундун чыгып кетүүсү	muundun ʧɪgɪp ketyysy
to dislocate (vt)	чыгарып алуу	ʧɪgarɪp aluu
fracture	сынуу	sɪnuu
to have a fracture	сындырып алуу	sɪndɪrɪp aluu
cut (e.g., paper ~)	кесилген жер	kesilgen ʤer
to cut oneself	кесип алуу	kesip aluu
bleeding	кан кетүү	kan ketyy
burn (injury)	күйүк	kyjyk
to get burned	күйгүзүп алуу	kyjgyzyp aluu
to prick (vt)	саюу	sajʉu
to prick oneself	сайып алуу	sajɪp aluu
to injure (vt)	кокустатып алуу	kokustatɪp aluu
injury	кокустатып алуу	kokustatɪp aluu
wound	жара	ʤara
trauma	жаракат	ʤarakat
to be delirious	жөлүү	ʤɵlyy
to stutter (vi)	кекечтенүү	kekeʧtenyy
sunstroke	күн өтүү	kyn ɵtyy

70. Symptoms. Treatments. Part 2

pain, ache	оору	ooru
splinter (in foot, etc.)	тикен	tiken
sweat (perspiration)	тер	ter
to sweat (perspire)	тердөө	terdøø
vomiting	кусуу	kusuu
convulsions	тарамыш карышуусу	taramɪʃ karɪʃuusu
pregnant (adj)	кош бойлуу	koʃ bojluu
to be born	төрөлүү	tørølyy

delivery, labor	төрөт	tørøt
to deliver (~ a baby)	төрөө	tørøø
abortion	бойдон түшүрүү	bojdon tyʃyryy

breathing, respiration	дем алуу	dem aluu
in-breath (inhalation)	дем алуу	dem aluu
out-breath (exhalation)	дем чыгаруу	dem tʃıgaruu
to exhale (breathe out)	дем чыгаруу	dem tʃıgaruu
to inhale (vi)	дем алуу	dem aluu

disabled person	майып	majıp
cripple	мунжу	mundʒu
drug addict	баңги	baŋgi

deaf (adj)	дүлөй	dyløj
mute (adj)	дудук	duduk
deaf mute (adj)	дудук	duduk

mad, insane (adj)	жин тийген	dʒin tijgen
madman (demented person)	жинди чалыш	dʒindi tʃalıʃ
madwoman	жинди чалыш	dʒindi tʃalıʃ
to go insane	мээси айныган	meesi ajnıgan

gene	ген	gen
immunity	иммунитет	immunitet
hereditary (adj)	тукум куучулук	tukum kuutʃuluk
congenital (adj)	тубаса	tubasa

virus	вирус	virus
microbe	микроб	mikrob
bacterium	бактерия	bakterija
infection	жугуштуу илдет	dʒuguʃtuu ildet

71. Symptoms. Treatments. Part 3

| hospital | оорукана | oorukana |
| patient | бейтап | bejtap |

diagnosis	дарт аныктоо	dart anıktoo
cure	дарылоо	darıloo
medical treatment	дарылоо	darıloo
to get treatment	дарылануу	darılanuu
to treat (~ a patient)	дарылоо	darıloo
to nurse (look after)	кароо	karoo
care (nursing ~)	кароо	karoo

operation, surgery	операция	operatsija
to bandage (head, limb)	жараны таңуу	dʒaranı taŋuu
bandaging	таңуу	taŋuu

vaccination	эмдөө	emdøø
to vaccinate (vt)	эмдөө	emdøø
injection, shot	ийне салуу	ijne saluu
to give an injection	ийне сайдыруу	iine saidiruu
attack	оору кармап калуу	ooru karmap kaluu
amputation	кесүү	kesyy
to amputate (vt)	кесип таштоо	kesip taʃtoo
coma	кома	koma
to be in a coma	комада болуу	komada boluu
intensive care	реанимация	reanimatsija
to recover (~ from flu)	сакаюу	sakajʉu
condition (patient's ~)	абал	abal
consciousness	эсинде	esinde
memory (faculty)	эс тутум	es tutum
to pull out (tooth)	тишти жулуу	tiʃti dʒuluu
filling	пломба	plomba
to fill (a tooth)	пломба салуу	plomba saluu
hypnosis	гипноз	gipnoz
to hypnotize (vt)	гипноз кылуу	gipnoz kıluu

72. Doctors

doctor	доктур	doktur
nurse	медсестра	medsestra
personal doctor	жекелик доктур	dʒekelik doktur
dentist	тиш доктур	tiʃ doktur
eye doctor	көз доктур	køz doktur
internist	терапевт	terapevt
surgeon	хирург	χirurg
psychiatrist	психиатр	psiχiatr
pediatrician	педиатр	pediatr
psychologist	психолог	psiχolog
gynecologist	гинеколог	ginekolog
cardiologist	кардиолог	kardiolog

73. Medicine. Drugs. Accessories

medicine, drug	дары-дармек	darı-darmek
remedy	дары	darı
to prescribe (vt)	жазып берүү	dʒazıp beryy
prescription	рецепт	retsept
tablet, pill	таблетка	tabletka

ointment	май	maj
ampule	ампула	ampula
mixture, solution	аралашма	aralaʃma
syrup	сироп	sirop
capsule	пилюля	piłɥłʲa
powder	күкүм	kykym
gauze bandage	бинт	bint
cotton wool	пахта	paχta
iodine	йод	jod
Band-Aid	лейкопластырь	lejkoplastɪrʲ
eyedropper	дары тамызгыч	darɪ tamɪzgɪtʃ
thermometer	градусник	gradusnik
syringe	шприц	ʃprits
wheelchair	майып арабасы	majɪp arabası
crutches	колтук таяк	koltuk tajak
painkiller	оору сездирбөөчү дары	ooru sezdirbøøtʃy darɪ
laxative	ич алдыруучу дары	itʃ aldıruutʃu darɪ
spirits (ethanol)	спирт	spirt
medicinal herbs	дары чөптөр	darɪ tʃøptør
herbal (~ tea)	чөп чайы	tʃøp tʃajı

74. Smoking. Tobacco products

tobacco	тамеки	tameki
cigarette	чылым	tʃılım
cigar	чылым	tʃılım
pipe	трубка	trubka
pack (of cigarettes)	пачке	patʃke
matches	ширеңке	ʃireŋke
matchbox	ширеңке кутусу	ʃireŋke kutusu
lighter	зажигалка	zadʒigalka
ashtray	күл салгыч	kyl salgɪtʃ
cigarette case	портсигар	portsigar
cigarette holder	мундштук	mundʃtuk
filter (cigarette tip)	фильтр	filʲtr
to smoke (vi, vt)	тамеки тартуу	tameki tartuu
to light a cigarette	күйгүзүп алуу	kyjgyzyp aluu
smoking	чылым чегүү	tʃılım tʃegyy
smoker	тамекичи	tamekitʃi
stub, butt (of cigarette)	чылым калдыгы	tʃılım kaldıgı
smoke, fumes	түтүн	tytyn
ash	күл	kyl

HUMAN HABITAT

City

city, town	шаар	ʃaar
capital city	борбор	borbor
village	кыштак	kɯʃtak
city map	шаардын планы	ʃaardɯn planɯ
downtown	шаардын борбору	ʃaardɯn borboru
suburb	шаардын чет жакасы	ʃaardɯn tʃet dʒakasɯ
suburban (adj)	шаардын чет жакасындагы	ʃaardɯn tʃet dʒakasɯndagɯ
outskirts	чет-жака	tʃet-dʒaka
environs (suburbs)	чет-жака	tʃet-dʒaka
city block	квартал	kvartal
residential block (area)	турак-жай кварталы	turak-dʒaj kvartalɯ
traffic	көчө кыймылы	køtʃø kɯjmɯlɯ
traffic lights	светофор	svetofor
public transportation	шаар транспорту	ʃaar transportu
intersection	кесилиш	kesiliʃ
crosswalk	жөө жүрүүчүлөр жолу	dʒøø dʒyryytʃylør dʒolu
pedestrian underpass	жер астындагы жол	dʒer astɯndagɯ dʒol
to cross (~ the street)	жолду өтүү	dʒoldu øtyy
pedestrian	жөө жүрүүчү	dʒøø dʒyryytʃy
sidewalk	жанжол	dʒandʒol
bridge	көпүрө	køpyrø
embankment (river walk)	жээк жол	dʒeek dʒol
fountain	фонтан	fontan
allée (garden walkway)	аллея	alleja
park	сейил багы	sejil bagɯ
boulevard	бульвар	bulʲvar
square	аянт	ajant
avenue (wide street)	проспект	prospekt
street	көчө	køtʃø
side street	чолок көчө	tʃolok køtʃø
dead end	түюк көчө	tujɯk køtʃø
house	үй	yj

building	имарат	imarat
skyscraper	көк тиреген көп кабаттуу үй	kök tiregen köp kabattuu yj

facade	үйдүн алды	yjdyn aldı
roof	чатыр	tʃatır
window	терезе	tereze
arch	түркүк	tyrkyk
column	мамы	mamı
corner	бурч	burtʃ

store window	көрсөтмө айнек үкөк	körsötmö ajnek ykök
signboard (store sign, etc.)	көрнөк	körnök
poster (e.g., playbill)	афиша	afiʃa
advertising poster	көрнөк-жарнак	körnök-dʒarnak
billboard	жарнамалык такта	dʒarnamalık takta

garbage, trash	таштанды	taʃtandı
trash can (public ~)	таштанды челек	taʃtandı tʃelek
to litter (vi)	таштоо	taʃtoo
garbage dump	таштанды үйүлгөн жер	taʃtandı yjylgön dʒer

phone booth	телефон будкасы	telefon budkası
lamppost	чырак мамы	tʃırak mamı
bench (park ~)	отургуч	oturgutʃ

police officer	полиция кызматкери	politsija kızmatkeri
police	полиция	politsija
beggar	кайырчы	kajırtʃı
homeless (n)	селсаяк	selsajak

76. Urban institutions

store	дүкөн	dykön
drugstore, pharmacy	дарыкана	darıkana
eyeglass store	оптика	optika
shopping mall	соода борбору	sooda borboru
supermarket	супермаркет	supermarket

bakery	нан дүкөнү	nan dyköny
baker	навайчы	navajtʃı
pastry shop	кондитердик дүкөн	konditerdik dykön
grocery store	азык-түлүк	azık-tylyk
butcher shop	эт дүкөнү	et dyköny

produce store	жашылча дүкөнү	dʒaʃıltʃa dyköny
market	базар	bazar

coffee house	кофекана	kofekana
restaurant	ресторан	restoran

pub, bar	сыракана	sırakana
pizzeria	пиццерия	pitʃerija
hair salon	чач тарач	tʃatʃ taratʃ
post office	почта	poʧta
dry cleaners	химиялык тазалоо	χimijalık tazaloo
photo studio	фотоателье	fotoatelje
shoe store	бут кийим дүкөнү	but kijim dykøny
bookstore	китеп дүкөнү	kitep dykøny
sporting goods store	спорт буюмдар дүкөнү	sport bujumdar dykøny
clothes repair shop	кийим ондоочу жай	kijim ondootʃu dʒaj
formal wear rental	кийимди ижарага берүү	kijimdi idʒaraga beryy
video rental store	тасмаларды ижарага берүү	tasmalardı idʒaraga beryy
circus	цирк	tsırk
zoo	зоопарк	zoopark
movie theater	кинотеатр	kinoteatr
museum	музей	muzej
library	китепкана	kitepkana
theater	театр	teatr
opera (opera house)	опера	opera
nightclub	түнкү клуб	tynky klub
casino	казино	kazino
mosque	мечит	metʃit
synagogue	синагога	sinagoga
cathedral	чоң чиркөө	tʃoŋ tʃirkøø
temple	ибадаткана	ibadatkana
church	чиркөө	tʃirkøø
college	коллеж	kolledʒ
university	университет	universitet
school	мектеп	mektep
prefecture	префектура	prefektura
city hall	мэрия	merija
hotel	мейманкана	mejmankana
bank	банк	bank
embassy	элчилик	eltʃilik
travel agency	турагенттиги	turagenttigi
information office	маалымат бюросу	maalımat bʉrosu
currency exchange	алмаштыруу пункту	almaʃtıruu punktu
subway	метро	metro
hospital	оорукана	oorukana
gas station	май куюучу станция	maj kujuutʃu stantsija
parking lot	унаа токтоочу жай	unaa toktootʃu dʒaj

77. Urban transportation

bus	автобус	avtobus
streetcar	трамвай	tramvaj
trolley bus	троллейбус	trollejbus
route (of bus, etc.)	каттам	kattam
number (e.g., bus ~)	номер	nomer
to go by ...	... жүрүү	... dʒyryy
to get on (~ the bus)	... отуруу	... oturuu
to get off ...	... түшүп калуу	... tyʃyp kaluu
stop (e.g., bus ~)	аялдама	ajaldama
next stop	кийинки аялдама	kijinki ajaldama
terminus	акыркы аялдама	akırkı ajaldama
schedule	ырааттама	ıraattama
to wait (vt)	күтүү	kytyy
ticket	билет	bilet
fare	билеттин баасы	bilettin baası
cashier (ticket seller)	кассир	kassir
ticket inspection	текшерүү	tekʃeryy
ticket inspector	текшерүүчү	tekʃeryytʃy
to be late (for ...)	кечигүү	ketʃigyy
to miss (~ the train, etc.)	кечигип калуу	ketʃigip kaluu
to be in a hurry	шашуу	ʃaʃuu
taxi, cab	такси	taksi
taxi driver	такси айдоочу	taksi ajdootʃu
by taxi	таксиде	takside
taxi stand	такси токтоочу жай	taksi toktootʃu dʒaj
to call a taxi	такси чакыруу	taksi tʃakıruu
to take a taxi	такси кармоо	taksi karmoo
traffic	көчө кыймылы	køtʃø kıjmılı
traffic jam	тыгын	tıgın
rush hour	кызуу маал	kızuu maal
to park (vi)	токтотуу	toktotuu
to park (vt)	машинаны жайлаштыруу	maʃinanı dʒajlaʃtıruu
parking lot	унаа токтоочу жай	unaa toktootʃu dʒaj
subway	метро	metro
station	бекет	beket
to take the subway	метродо жүрүү	metrodo dʒyryy
train	поезд	poezd
train station	вокзал	vokzal

78. Sightseeing

monument	эстелик	estelik
fortress	чеп	ʧøp
palace	сарай	saraj
castle	сепил	sepil
tower	мунара	munara
mausoleum	күмбөз	kymbøz

architecture	архитектура	arχitektura
medieval (adj)	орто кылымдык	orto kılımdık
ancient (adj)	байыркы	bajırkı
national (adj)	улуттук	uluttuk
famous (monument, etc.)	таанымал	taanımal

tourist	турист	turist
guide (person)	гид	gid
excursion, sightseeing tour	экскурсия	ekskursija
to show (vt)	көрсөтүү	kørsøtyy
to tell (vt)	айтып берүү	ajtıp beryy

to find (vt)	табуу	tabuu
to get lost (lose one's way)	адашып кетүү	adaʃıp ketyy
map (e.g., subway ~)	схема	sχema
map (e.g., city ~)	план	plan

souvenir, gift	асембелек	asembelek
gift shop	асембелек дүкөнү	asembelek dykøny
to take pictures	сүрөткө тартуу	syrøtkø tartuu
to have one's picture taken	сүрөткө түшүү	syrøtkø tyʃyy

79. Shopping

to buy (purchase)	сатып алуу	satıp aluu
purchase	сатып алуу	satıp aluu
to go shopping	сатып алууга чыгуу	satıp aluuga ʧıguu
shopping	базарчылоо	bazarʧıloo

| to be open (ab. store) | иштөө | iʃtøø |
| to be closed | жабылуу | dʒabıluu |

footwear, shoes	бут кийим	but kijim
clothes, clothing	кийим-кече	kijim-keʧe
cosmetics	упа-эндик	upa-endik
food products	азык-түлүк	azık-tylyk
gift, present	белек	belek

| salesman | сатуучу | satuuʧu |
| saleswoman | сатуучу кыз | satuuʧu kız |

check out, cash desk	касса	kassa
mirror	күзгү	kyzgy
counter (store ~)	прилавок	prilavok
fitting room	кийим ченөөчү бөлмө	kijim ʧenøøʧy bølmø

to try on	кийим ченөө	kijim ʧenøø
to fit (ab. dress, etc.)	ылайык келүү	ɪlajɪk kelyy
to like (I like …)	жактыруу	dʒaktɪruu

price	баа	baa
price tag	баа	baa
to cost (vt)	туруу	turuu
How much?	Канча?	kanʧa?
discount	арзандатуу	arzandatuu

inexpensive (adj)	кымбат эмес	kɪmbat emes
cheap (adj)	арзан	arzan
expensive (adj)	кымбат	kɪmbat
It's expensive	Бул кымбат	bul kɪmbat

rental (n)	ижара	idʒara
to rent (~ a tuxedo)	ижарага алуу	idʒaraga aluu
credit (trade credit)	насыя	nasɪja
on credit (adv)	насыяга алуу	nasɪjaga aluu

80. Money

money	акча	akʧa
currency exchange	алмаштыруу	almaʃtɪruu
exchange rate	курс	kurs
ATM	банкомат	bankomat
coin	тыйын	tɪjɪn

| dollar | доллар | dollar |
| euro | евро | evro |

lira	италиялык лира	italijalɪk lira
Deutschmark	немис маркасы	nemis markasɪ
franc	франк	frank
pound sterling	фунт стерлинг	funt sterling
yen	йена	jena

debt	карыз	karɪz
debtor	карыздар	karɪzdar
to lend (money)	карызга берүү	karɪzga beryy
to borrow (vi, vt)	карызга алуу	karɪzga aluu

bank	банк	bank
account	эсеп	esep
to deposit (vt)	салуу	saluu

to deposit into the account	эсепке акча салуу	esepke aktʃa saluu
to withdraw (vt)	эсептен акча чыгаруу	esepten aktʃa tʃɪgaruu
credit card	насыя картасы	nasɪja kartasɪ
cash	накталай акча	nuktulaj alıtʃa
check	чек	tʃek
to write a check	чек жазып берүү	tʃek dʒazɪp beryy
checkbook	чек китепчеси	tʃek kiteptʃesi
wallet	намыян	namɪjan
change purse	капчык	kaptʃɪk
safe	сейф	sejf
heir	мураскер	murasker
inheritance	мурас	muras
fortune (wealth)	мүлк	mylk
lease	ижара	idʒara
rent (money)	батир акысы	batir akɪsɪ
to rent (sth from sb)	батирге алуу	batirge aluu
price	баа	baa
cost	баа	baa
sum	сумма	summa
to spend (vt)	коротуу	korotuu
expenses	чыгым	tʃɪgɪm
to economize (vi, vt)	үнөмдөө	ynømdøø
economical	сарамжал	saramdʒal
to pay (vi, vt)	төлөө	tøløø
payment	акы төлөө	akɪ tøløø
change (give the ~)	кайтарылган майда акча	kajtarɪlgan majda aktʃa
tax	салык	salɪk
fine	айып	ajɪp
to fine (vt)	айып пул салуу	ajɪp pul saluu

81. Post. Postal service

post office	почта	potʃta
mail (letters, etc.)	почта	potʃta
mailman	кат ташуучу	kat taʃuutʃu
opening hours	иш сааттары	iʃ saattarɪ
letter	кат	kat
registered letter	тапшырык кат	tapʃırık kat
postcard	открытка	otkrɪtka
telegram	телеграмма	telegramma

| package (parcel) | посылка | posılka |
| money transfer | акча которуу | aktʃa kotoruu |

to receive (vt)	алуу	aluu
to send (vt)	жөнөтүү	dʒønøtyy
sending	жөнөтүү	dʒønøtyy

address	дарек	darek
ZIP code	индекс	indeks
sender	жөнөтүүчү	dʒønøtyytʃy
receiver	алуучу	aluutʃu

| name (first name) | аты | atı |
| surname (last name) | фамилиясы | familijası |

postage rate	тариф	tarif
standard (adj)	жөнөкөй	dʒønøkøj
economical (adj)	үнөмдүү	ynømdyy

weight	салмак	salmak
to weigh (~ letters)	таразалоо	tarazaloo
envelope	конверт	konvert
postage stamp	марка	marka
to stamp an envelope	марка жабыштыруу	marka dʒabıʃtıruu

Dwelling. House. Home

82. House. Dwelling

house	үй	yj
at home (adv)	үйүндө	yjyndø
yard	эшик	eʃik
fence (iron ~)	тосмо	tosmo
brick (n)	кыш	kıʃ
brick (as adj)	кыштан	kıʃtan
stone (n)	таш	taʃ
stone (as adj)	таш	taʃ
concrete (n)	бетон	beton
concrete (as adj)	бетон	beton
new (new-built)	жаңы	dʒaŋı
old (adj)	эски	eski
decrepit (house)	эскирген	eskirgen
modern (adj)	заманбап	zamanbap
multistory (adj)	көп кабаттуу	køp kabattuu
tall (~ building)	бийик	bijik
floor, story	кабат	kabat
single-story (adj)	бир кабаттуу	bir kabat
1st floor	ылдыйкы этаж	ıldıjkı etadʒ
top floor	үстүңкү этаж	ystyŋky etadʒ
roof	чатыр	tʃatır
chimney	мор	mor
roof tiles	чатыр карапа	tʃatır karapa
tiled (adj)	карапалуу	karapaluu
attic (storage place)	чердак	tʃerdak
window	терезе	tereze
glass	айнек	ajnek
window ledge	текче	tektʃe
shutters	терезе жапкычы	tereze dʒapkıtʃı
wall	дубал	dubal
balcony	балкон	balkon
downspout	суу аккан түтүк	suu akkan tytyk
upstairs (to be ~)	өйдө	øjdø
to go upstairs	көтөрүлүү	køtørylyy

| to come down (the stairs) | ылдый түшүү | ıldıj tyʃyy |
| to move (to new premises) | көчүү | køtʃyy |

83. House. Entrance. Lift

entrance	подъезд	podʰjezd
stairs (stairway)	тепкич	tepkitʃ
steps	тепкичтер	tepkitʃter
banister	тосмо	tosmo
lobby (hotel ~)	холл	χoll

mailbox	почта ящиги	potʃta jaʃtʃigi
garbage can	таштанды челеги	taʃtandı tʃelegi
trash chute	таштанды түтүгү	taʃtandı tytygy

elevator	лифт	lift
freight elevator	жүк ташуучу лифт	dʒyk taʃuutʃu lift
elevator cage	кабина	kabina
to take the elevator	лифтке түшүү	liftke tyʃyy

apartment	батир	batir
residents (~ of a building)	жашоочулар	dʒaʃootʃular
neighbor (masc.)	кошуна	koʃuna
neighbor (fem.)	кошуна	koʃuna
neighbors	кошуналар	koʃunalar

84. House. Doors. Locks

door	эшик	eʃik
gate (vehicle ~)	дарбаза	darbaza
handle, doorknob	тутка	tutka
to unlock (unbolt)	кулпусун ачуу	kulpusun atʃuu
to open (vt)	ачуу	atʃuu
to close (vt)	жабуу	dʒabuu

key	ачкыч	atʃkıtʃ
bunch (of keys)	ачкычтар тизмеси	atʃkıtʃtar tizmesi
to creak (door, etc.)	кычыратуу	kıtʃıratuu
creak	чыйкылдоо	tʃıjkıldoo
hinge (door ~)	петля	petlʲa
doormat	килемче	kilemtʃe

door lock	кулпу	kulpu
keyhole	кулпу тешиги	kulpu teʃigi
crossbar (sliding bar)	бекитме	bekitme
door latch	тээк	teek
padlock	асма кулпу	asma kulpu
to ring (~ the door bell)	чалуу	tʃaluu

ringing (sound)	шыңгыраш	ʃıŋgıraʃ
doorbell	коңуроо	konguroo
doorbell button	коңуроо баскычы	konguroo baskıtʃı
knock (at the door)	такылдатуу	takıldatuu
to knock (vi)	такылдатуу	takıldatuu
code	код	kod
combination lock	код кулпусу	kod kulpusu
intercom	домофон	domofon
number (on the door)	номер	nomer
doorplate	тактача	taktatʃa
peephole	көзче	køztʃø

85. Country house

village	кыштак	kıʃtak
vegetable garden	чарбак	tʃarbak
fence	тосмо	tosmo
picket fence	кашаа	kaʃaa
wicket gate	каалга	kaalga
granary	кампа	kampa
root cellar	ороо	oroo
shed (garden ~)	сарай	saraj
water well	кудук	kuduk
stove (wood-fired ~)	меш	meʃ
to stoke the stove	меш жагуу	meʃ dʒaguu
firewood	отун	otun
log (firewood)	бир кертим жыгач	bir kertim dʒıgatʃ
veranda	веранда	veranda
deck (terrace)	терасса	terassa
stoop (front steps)	босого	bosogo
swing (hanging seat)	селкинчек	selkintʃek

86. Castle. Palace

castle	сепил	sepil
palace	сарай	saraj
fortress	чеп	tʃep
wall (round castle)	дубал	dubal
tower	мунара	munara
keep, donjon	баш мунара	baʃ munara
portcullis	көтөрүлүүчү дарбаза	køtørylyytʃy darbaza
underground passage	жер астындагы жол	dʒer astındagı dʒol

moat	сепил аңгеги	ɵɵpil aŋgegi
chain	чынжыр	tʃɯndʒɯr
arrow loop	атуучу тешик	atuutʃu teʃik

magnificent (adj)	сонун	sonun
majestic (adj)	даңазалуу	daŋazaluu
impregnable (adj)	бекем чеп	bekem tʃep
medieval (adj)	орто кылымдык	orto kɯlɯmdɯk

87. Apartment

apartment	батир	batir
room	бөлмө	bølmø
bedroom	уктоочу бөлмө	uktootʃu bølmø
dining room	ашкана	aʃkana
living room	конок үйү	konok yjy
study (home office)	иш бөлмөсү	iʃ bølmøsy

entry room	кире бериш	kire beriʃ
bathroom (room with a bath or shower)	ванная	vannaja
half bath	даараткана	daaratkana

ceiling	шып	ʃɯp
floor	пол	pol
corner	бурч	burtʃ

88. Apartment. Cleaning

| to clean (vi, vt) | жыйноо | dʒɯjnoo |
| to put away (to stow) | жыйноо | dʒɯjnoo |

dust	чаң	tʃaŋ
dusty (adj)	чаң баскан	tʃaŋ baskan
to dust (vt)	чаң сүртүү	tʃaŋ syrtyy
vacuum cleaner	чаң соргуч	tʃaŋ sorgutʃ
to vacuum (vt)	чаң сордуруу	tʃaŋ sorduruu

| to sweep (vi, vt) | шыпыруу | ʃɯpɯruu |
| sweepings | шыпырынды | ʃɯpɯrɯndɯ |

| order | иреттелген | irettelgen |
| disorder, mess | чачылган | tʃatʃɯlgan |

mop	швабра	ʃvabra
dust cloth	чүпүрөк	tʃypyrøk
short broom	шыпыргы	ʃɯpɯrgɯ
dustpan	калак	kalak

89. Furniture. Interior

furniture	эмерек	emerek
table	стол	stol
chair	стул	stul
bed	керебет	kerebet
couch, sofa	диван	divan
armchair	олпок отургуч	olpok oturguʧ
bookcase	китеп шкафы	kitep ʃkafı
shelf	текче	tektʃe
wardrobe	шкаф	ʃkaf
coat rack (wall-mounted ~)	кийим илгич	kijim ilgiʧ
coat stand	кийим илгич	kijim ilgiʧ
bureau, dresser	комод	komod
coffee table	журнал столу	dʒurnal stolu
mirror	күзгү	kyzgy
carpet	килем	kilem
rug, small carpet	килемче	kilemtʃe
fireplace	очок	oʧok
candle	шам	ʃam
candlestick	шамдал	ʃamdal
drapes	парда	parda
wallpaper	туш кагаз	tuʃ kagaz
blinds (jalousie)	жалюзи	dʒaldʒuzi
table lamp	стол чырагы	stol ʧıragı
wall lamp (sconce)	чырак	ʧırak
floor lamp	торшер	torʃer
chandelier	асма шам	asma ʃam
leg (of chair, table)	бут	but
armrest	чыканак такооч	ʧıkanak takooʧ
back (backrest)	жөлөнгүч	dʒøløngyʧ
drawer	суурма	suurma

90. Bedding

bedclothes	шейшеп	ʃejʃep
pillow	жаздык	dʒazdık
pillowcase	жаздык кап	dʒazdık kap
duvet, comforter	жууркан	dʒuurkan
sheet	шейшеп	ʃejʃep
bedspread	жапкыч	dʒapkıʧ

91. Kitchen

kitchen	ашкана	aʃkana
gas	газ	gaz
gas stove (range)	газ плитасы	gaz plitası
electric stove	электр плитасы	elektr plitası
oven	духовка	duχovka
microwave oven	микротолкун меши	mikrotolkun meʃi

refrigerator	муздаткыч	muzdatkıtʃ
freezer	тоңдургуч	toŋdurgutʃ
dishwasher	идиш жуучу машина	idiʃ dʒuutʃu maʃina

meat grinder	эт туурагыч	et tuuragıtʃ
juicer	шире сыккыч	ʃire sıkkıtʃ
toaster	тостер	toster
mixer	миксер	mikser

coffee machine	кофе кайнаткыч	kofe kajnatkıtʃ
coffee pot	кофе кайнатуучу идиш	kofe kajnatuutʃu idiʃ
coffee grinder	кофе майдалагыч	kofe majdalagıtʃ

kettle	чайнек	tʃajnek
teapot	чайнек	tʃajnek
lid	капкак	kapkak
tea strainer	чыпка	tʃıpka

spoon	кашык	kaʃık
teaspoon	чай кашык	tʃaj kaʃık
soup spoon	аш кашык	aʃ kaʃık
fork	вилка	vilka
knife	бычак	bıtʃak

tableware (dishes)	идиш-аяк	idiʃ-ajak
plate (dinner ~)	табак	tabak
saucer	табак	tabak

shot glass	рюмка	rʉmka
glass (tumbler)	ыстакан	ıstakan
cup	чөйчөк	tʃøjtʃøk

sugar bowl	кум шекер салгыч	kum ʃeker salgıtʃ
salt shaker	туз салгыч	tuz salgıtʃ
pepper shaker	мурч салгыч	murtʃ salgıtʃ
butter dish	май салгыч	maj salgıtʃ

stock pot (soup pot)	мискей	miskej
frying pan (skillet)	табак	tabak
ladle	чөмүч	tʃømytʃ
colander	депкир	depkir
tray (serving ~)	батыныс	batınıs

bottle	бөтөлкө	bøtølkø
jar (glass)	банка	banka
can	банка	banka

bottle opener	ачкыч	atʃkɪtʃ
can opener	ачкыч	atʃkɪtʃ
corkscrew	штопор	ʃtopor
filter	чыпка	tʃɪpka
to filter (vt)	чыпкалоо	tʃɪpkaloo

| trash, garbage (food waste, etc.) | таштанды | taʃtandɪ |
| trash can (kitchen ~) | таштанды чака | taʃtandɪ tʃaka |

92. Bathroom

bathroom	ванная	vannaja
water	суу	suu
faucet	чорго	tʃorgo
hot water	ысык суу	ɪsɪk suu
cold water	муздак суу	muzdak suu

toothpaste	тиш пастасы	tiʃ pastasɪ
to brush one's teeth	тиш жуу	tiʃ dʒuu
toothbrush	тиш щёткасы	tiʃ ʃtʃotkasɪ

to shave (vi)	кырынуу	kɪrɪnuu
shaving foam	кырынуу үчүн көбүк	kɪrɪnuu ytʃyn købyk
razor	устара	ustara

to wash (one's hands, etc.)	жуу	dʒuu
to take a bath	жуунуу	dʒuunuu
shower	душ	duʃ
to take a shower	душка түшүү	duʃka tyʃyy
bathtub	ванна	vanna
toilet (toilet bowl)	унитаз	unitaz
sink (washbasin)	раковина	rakovina

| soap | самын | samɪn |
| soap dish | самын салгыч | samɪn salgɪtʃ |

sponge	губка	gubka
shampoo	шампунь	ʃampunʲ
towel	сүлгү	sylgy
bathrobe	халат	χalat

laundry (laundering)	кир жуу	kir dʒuu
washing machine	кир жуучу машина	kir dʒuutʃu maʃina
to do the laundry	кир жуу	kir dʒuu
laundry detergent	кир жуучу порошок	kir dʒuutʃu poroʃok

93. Household appliances

TV set	сыналгы	sınalgı
tape recorder	магнитофон	magnitofon
VCR (video recorder)	видеомагнитофон	videomagnitofon
radio	үналгы	ynalgı
player (CD, MP3, etc.)	плеер	pleer
video projector	видеопроектор	videoproektor
home movie theater	үй кинотеатры	yj kinoteatrı
DVD player	DVD ойноткуч	dividi ojnotkuʧ
amplifier	күчөткүч	kyʧøtkyʧ
video game console	оюн приставкасы	ojun pristavkası
video camera	видеокамера	videokamera
camera (photo)	фотоаппарат	fotoapparat
digital camera	санарип камерасы	sanarip kamerası
vacuum cleaner	чаң соргуч	ʧaŋ sorguʧ
iron (e.g., steam ~)	үтүк	ytyk
ironing board	үтүктөөчү тактай	ytyktøøʧy taktaj
telephone	телефон	telefon
cell phone	мобилдик	mobildik
typewriter	машинка	maʃinka
sewing machine	кийим тигүүчү машинка	kijim tigyyʧy maʃinka
microphone	микрофон	mikrofon
headphones	кулакчын	kulakʧın
remote control (TV)	пульт	pulʲt
CD, compact disc	CD, компакт-диск	sidi, kompakt-disk
cassette, tape	кассета	kasseta
vinyl record	пластинка	plastinka

94. Repairs. Renovation

renovations	ремонт	remont
to renovate (vt)	ремонт жасоо	remont dʒasoo
to repair, to fix (vt)	оңдоо	oŋdoo
to put in order	иретке келтирүү	iretke keltiryy
to redo (do again)	кайра жасатуу	kajra dʒasatuu
paint	сыр	sır
to paint (~ a wall)	боео	boeo
house painter	боекчу	boektʃu
paintbrush	кисть	kistʲ
whitewash	акиташ	akitaʃ
to whitewash (vt)	актоо	aktoo

wallpaper	туш кагаз	tuʃ kagaz
to wallpaper (vt)	туш кагаз менен чаптоо	tuʃ kagaz menen ʧaptoo
varnish	лак	lak
to varnish (vt)	лак менен жабуу	lak menen ʤabuu

95. Plumbing

water	суу	suu
hot water	ысык суу	ɪsɪk suu
cold water	муздак суу	muzdak suu
faucet	чорго	ʧorgo

drop (of water)	тамчы	tamʧɪ
to drip (vi)	тамчылоо	tamʧɪloo
to leak (ab. pipe)	агуу	aguu
leak (pipe ~)	суу өтүү	suu øtyy
puddle	көлчүк	kølʧyk

pipe	түтүк	tytyk
valve (e.g., ball ~)	чорго	ʧorgo
to be clogged up	тыгылуу	tɪgɪluu

tools	аспаптар	aspaptar
adjustable wrench	бурама ачкыч	burama aʧkɪʧ
to unscrew (lid, filter, etc.)	бурап чыгаруу	burap ʧɪgaruu
to screw (tighten)	бурап бекитүү	burap bekityy

to unclog (vt)	тазалоо	tazaloo
plumber	сантехник	santeχnik
basement	жер асты	ʤer astɪ
sewerage (system)	канализация	kanalizatsija

96. Fire. Conflagration

fire (accident)	өрт	ørt
flame	жалын	ʤalɪn
spark	учкун	uʧkun
smoke (from fire)	түтүн	tytyn
torch (flaming stick)	шамана	ʃamana
campfire	от	ot

gas, gasoline	күйүүчү май	kyjyyʧy may
kerosene (type of fuel)	керосин	kerosin
flammable (adj)	күйүүчү	kyjyyʧy
explosive (adj)	жарылуу коркунучу	ʤarɪluu korkunuʧu
NO SMOKING	ТАМЕКИ ЧЕГҮҮГӨ БОЛБОЙТ!	tameki ʧegyygø bolbojt!
safety	коопсуз	koopsuz

danger	коркунуч	kɔrkunutʃ
dangerous (adj)	кооптуу	kooptuu
to catch fire	от алуу	ot aluu
explosion	жарылуу	dʒarıluu
to set fire	өрттөө	ørttøø
arsonist	өрттөөчү	ørttøøtʃy
arson	өрттөө	ørttøø
to blaze (vi)	жалындап күйүү	dʒalındap kyjyy
to burn (be on fire)	күйүү	kyjyy
to burn down	күйүп кетүү	kyjyp ketyy
to call the fire department	өрт өчүргүчтөрдү чакыруу	ørt øtʃyrgytʃtørdy tʃakıruu
firefighter, fireman	өрт өчүргүч	ørt øtʃyrgytʃ
fire truck	өрт өчүрүүчү машина	ørt øtʃyryytʃy maʃina
fire department	өрт өчүрүү командасы	ørt øtʃyryy komandası
fire truck ladder	өрт өчүрүүчү шаты	ørt øtʃyryytʃy ʃatı
fire hose	шланг	ʃlang
fire extinguisher	өрт өчүргүч	ørt øtʃyrgytʃ
helmet	каска	kaska
siren	сирена	sirena
to cry (for help)	айгай салуу	ajgaj saluu
to call for help	жардамга чакыруу	dʒardamga tʃakıruu
rescuer	куткаруучу	kutkaruutʃu
to rescue (vt)	куткаруу	kutkaruu
to arrive (vi)	келүү	kelyy
to extinguish (vt)	өчүрүү	øtʃyryy
water	суу	suu
sand	кум	kum
ruins (destruction)	уранды	urandı
to collapse (building, etc.)	уроо	uroo
to fall down (vi)	кулоо	kuloo
to cave in (ceiling, floor)	урап түшүү	urap tuʃyy
piece of debris	сыныk	sınık
ash	күл	kyl
to suffocate (die)	тумчугуу	tumtʃuguu
to be killed (perish)	өлүү	ølyy

HUMAN ACTIVITIES

Job. Business. Part 1

97. Banking

bank	банк	bank
branch (of bank, etc.)	бөлүм	bølym
bank clerk, consultant	кеңешчи	keŋeʃʧi
manager (director)	башкаруучу	baʃkaruutʃu
bank account	эсеп	esep
account number	эсеп номери	esep nomeri
checking account	учурдагы эсеп	utʃurdagı esep
savings account	топтолмо эсеп	toptolmo esep
to open an account	эсеп ачуу	esep atʃuu
to close the account	эсеп жабуу	esep dʒabuu
to deposit into the account	эсепке акча салуу	esepke aktʃa saluu
to withdraw (vt)	эсептен акча чыгаруу	esepten aktʃa tʃıgaruu
deposit	аманат	amanat
to make a deposit	аманат кылуу	amanat kıluu
wire transfer	акча которуу	aktʃa kotoruu
to wire, to transfer	акча которуу	aktʃa kotoruu
sum	сумма	summa
How much?	Канча?	kantʃa?
signature	кол тамга	kol tamga
to sign (vt)	кол коюу	kol kojʉu
credit card	насыя картасы	nasıja kartası
code (PIN code)	код	kod
credit card number	насыя картанын номери	nasıja kartanın nomeri
ATM	банкомат	bankomat
check	чек	tʃek
to write a check	чек жазып берүү	tʃek dʒazıp beryy
checkbook	чек китепчеси	tʃek kiteptʃesi
loan (bank ~)	насыя	nasıja
to apply for a loan	насыя үчүн кайрылуу	nasıja ytʃyn kajrıluu

to get a loan	насыя алуу	nasıja aluu
to give a loan	насыя берүү	nasıja beryy
guarantee	кепилдик	kepildik

98. Telephone. Phone conversation

telephone	телефон	telefon
cell phone	мобилдик	mobildik
answering machine	автоматтык жооп берүүчү	avtomattık dʒoop beryytʃy

| to call (by phone) | чалуу | tʃaluu |
| phone call | чакыруу | tʃakıruu |

to dial a number	номер терүү	nomer teryy
Hello!	Алло!	allo!
to ask (vt)	суроо	suroo
to answer (vi, vt)	жооп берүү	dʒoop beryy

to hear (vt)	угуу	uguu
well (adv)	жакшы	dʒakʃı
not well (adv)	жаман	dʒaman
noises (interference)	ызы-чуу	ızı-tʃuu

receiver	трубка	trubka
to pick up (~ the phone)	трубканы алуу	trubkanı aluu
to hang up (~ the phone)	трубканы коюу	trubkanı kojʉu

busy (engaged)	бош эмес	boʃ emes
to ring (ab. phone)	шыңгыроо	ʃıŋgıroo
telephone book	телефондук китепче	telefonduk kiteptʃe

local (adj)	жергиликтүү	dʒergiliktyy
local call	жергиликтүү чакыруу	dʒergiliktyy tʃakıruu
long distance (~ call)	шаар аралык	ʃaar aralık
long-distance call	шаар аралык чакыруу	ʃaar aralık tʃakıruu
international (adj)	эл аралык	el aralık
international call	эл аралык чакыруу	el aralık tʃakıruu

99. Cell phone

cell phone	мобилдик	mobildik
display	дисплей	displej
button	баскыч	baskıtʃ
SIM card	SIM-карта	sim-karta

| battery | батарея | batareja |
| to be dead (battery) | зарядканын түгөнүүсү | zarʲadkanın tygønyysy |

charger	заряддоочу шайман	zarʲaddooʧu ʃajman
menu	меню	menʉ
settings	орнотуулар	ornotuular
tune (melody)	обон	obon
to select (vt)	тандоо	tandoo

calculator	калькулятор	kalʲkulʲator
voice mail	автоматтык жооп бергич	avtomattık dʒoop bergiʧ
alarm clock	ойготкуч	ojgotkuʧ
contacts	байланыштар	bajlanıʃtar

| SMS (text message) | SMS-кабар | esemes-kabar |
| subscriber | абонент | abonent |

100. Stationery

| ballpoint pen | калем сап | kalem sap |
| fountain pen | калем уч | kalem uʧ |

pencil	карандаш	karandaʃ
highlighter	маркер	marker
felt-tip pen	фломастер	flomaster

| notepad | дептерче | depterʧe |
| agenda (diary) | күндөлүк | kyndølyk |

ruler	сызгыч	sızgıʧ
calculator	калькулятор	kalʲkulʲator
eraser	өчүргүч	øʧyrgyʧ
thumbtack	кнопка	knopka
paper clip	кыскыч	kıskıʧ

glue	желим	dʒelim
stapler	степлер	stepler
hole punch	тешкич	teʃkiʧ
pencil sharpener	учтагыч	uʧtagıʧ

Job. Business. Part 2

101. Mass Media

newspaper	гезит	gezit
magazine	журнал	ʤurnal
press (printed media)	пресса	pressa
radio	үналгы	ynalgı
radio station	радио толкуну	radio tolkunu
television	телекөрсөтүү	telekørsøtyy
presenter, host	алып баруучу	alıp baruuʧu
newscaster	диктор	diktor
commentator	баяндамачы	bajandamaʧı
journalist	журналист	ʤurnalist
correspondent (reporter)	кабарчы	kabarʧı
press photographer	фотокорреспондент	fotokorrespondent
reporter	репортёр	reportior
editor	редактор	redaktor
editor-in-chief	башкы редактор	baʃkı redaktor
to subscribe (to ...)	жазылуу	ʤazıluu
subscription	жазылуу	ʤazıluu
subscriber	жазылуучу	ʤazıluuʧu
to read (vi, vt)	окуу	okuu
reader	окурман	okurman
circulation (of newspaper)	нуска	nuska
monthly (adj)	ай сайын	aj sajın
weekly (adj)	жума сайын	ʤuma sajın
issue (edition)	номер	nomer
new (~ issue)	жаңы	ʤaŋı
headline	баш аты	baʃ atı
short article	кыскача макала	kıskaʧa makala
column (regular article)	рубрика	rubrika
article	макала	makala
page	бет	bet
reportage, report	репортаж	reportaʤ
event (happening)	окуя	okuja
sensation (news)	дүң салуу	dyŋ saluu
scandal	жаңжал	ʤaŋʤal
scandalous (adj)	жаңжалчы	ʤaŋʤalʧı

great (~ scandal)	чуулгандуу	ʧuulganduu
show (e.g., cooking ~)	көрсөтүү	kørsøtyy
interview	интервью	intervjʉ
live broadcast	түз берүү	tyz beryy
channel	канал	kaнal

102. Agriculture

agriculture	дыйкан чарбачылык	dıjkan ʧarbaʧılık
peasant (masc.)	дыйкан	dıjkan
peasant (fem.)	дыйкан аял	dıjkan ajal
farmer	фермер	fermer

| tractor (farm ~) | трактор | traktor |
| combine, harvester | комбайн | kombajn |

plow	соко	soko
to plow (vi, vt)	жер айдоо	ʤer ajdoo
plowland	айдоо жер	ajdoo ʤer
furrow (in field)	жөөк	ʤøøk

to sow (vi, vt)	себүү	sebyy
seeder	сеялка	sejalka
sowing (process)	эгүү	egyy

| scythe | чалгы | ʧalgı |
| to mow, to scythe | чабуу | ʧabuu |

| spade (tool) | күрөк | kyrøk |
| to till (vt) | казуу | kazuu |

hoe	кетмен	ketmen
to hoe, to weed	отоо	otoo
weed (plant)	отоо чеп	otoo ʧøp

watering can	гүл челек	gyl ʧelek
to water (plants)	сугаруу	sugaruu
watering (act)	сугат	sugat

| pitchfork | айры | ajrı |
| rake | тырмоо | tırmoo |

fertilizer	жер семирткич	ʤer semirtkiʧ
to fertilize (vt)	жер семиртүү	ʤer semirtyy
manure (fertilizer)	кык	kık

field	талаа	talaa
meadow	шалбаа	ʃalbaa
vegetable garden	чарбак	ʧarbak
orchard (e.g., apple ~)	бакча	bakʧa

to graze (vi)	жайуу	dʒajдʒuu
herder (herdsman)	чабан	tʃaban
pasture	жайыт	dʒajıt
cattle breeding	мал чарбачылык	mal tʃarbatʃılık
sheep farming	кой чарбачылык	koj tʃarbatʃılık
plantation	плантация	plantatsija
row (garden bed ~s)	жөөк	dʒøøk
hothouse	күнөскана	kynøskana
drought (lack of rain)	кургакчылык	kurgaktʃılık
dry (~ summer)	кургак	kurgak
grain	дан эгиндери	dan eginderi
cereal crops	дан эгиндери	dan eginderi
to harvest, to gather	чаап алуу	tʃaap aluu
miller (person)	тегирменчи	tegirmentʃi
mill (e.g., gristmill)	тегирмен	tegirmen
to grind (grain)	майдалоо	majdaloo
flour	ун	un
straw	саман	saman

103. Building. Building process

construction site	курулуш	kuruluʃ
to build (vt)	куруу	kuruu
construction worker	куруучу	kuruutʃu
project	долбоор	dolboor
architect	архитектор	arχitektor
worker	жумушчу	dʒumuʃtʃu
foundation (of a building)	пайдубал	pajdubal
roof	чатыр	tʃatır
foundation pile	казык	kazık
wall	дубал	dubal
reinforcing bars	арматура	armatura
scaffolding	куруучу тепкичтер	kuruutʃu tepkitʃter
concrete	бетон	beton
granite	гранит	granit
stone	таш	taʃ
brick	кыш	kıʃ
sand	кум	kum
cement	цемент	tsement
plaster (for walls)	шыбак	ʃıbak

to plaster (vt)	шыбоо	ʃıboo
paint	сыр	sır
to paint (~ a wall)	боео	boeo
barrel	бочка	botʃka

crane	кран	kran
to lift, to hoist (vt)	көтөрүү	køtøryy
to lower (vt)	түшүрүү	tyʃyryy

bulldozer	бульдозер	bulʲdozer
excavator	экскаватор	ekskavator
scoop, bucket	ковш	kovʃ
to dig (excavate)	казуу	kazuu
hard hat	каска	kaska

Professions and occupations

104. Job search. Dismissal

job	иш	iʃ
staff (work force)	жамаат	dʒamaat
personnel	жамаат курамы	dʒamaat kuramı
career	мансап	mansap
prospects (chances)	перспектива	perspektiva
skills (mastery)	чеберчилик	tʃebertʃilik
selection (screening)	тандоо	tandoo
employment agency	кадрдык агенттиги	kadrdık agenttigi
résumé	таржымал	tardʒımal
job interview	аңгемелешүү	aŋgemeleʃyy
vacancy, opening	жумуш орун	dʒumuʃ orun
salary, pay	эмгек акы	emgek akı
fixed salary	маяна	majana
pay, compensation	акысын төлөө	akısın tøløø
position (job)	кызмат орун	kızmat orun
duty (of employee)	милдет	mildet
range of duties	милдеттенмелер	mildettenmeler
busy (I'm ~)	бош эмес	boʃ emes
to fire (dismiss)	бошотуу	boʃotuu
dismissal	бошотуу	boʃotuu
unemployment	жумушсуздук	dʒumuʃsuzduk
unemployed (n)	жумушсуз	dʒumuʃsuz
retirement	баwaракы	baarakı
to retire (from job)	ардактуу эс алууга чыгуу	ardaktuu es aluuga tʃıguu

105. Business people

director	директор	direktor
manager (director)	башкаруучу	baʃkaruutʃu
boss	башкаруучу	baʃkaruutʃu
superior	башчы	baʃtʃı
superiors	башчылар	baʃtʃılar

| president | президент | prezident |
| chairman | төрага | tøraga |

deputy (substitute)	орун басар	orun basar
assistant	жардамчы	ʤardamʧı
secretary	катчы	katʧı
personal assistant	жеке катчы	ʤeke katʧı

businessman	бизнесмен	biznesmen
entrepreneur	ишкер	iʃker
founder	негиздөөчү	negizdøøʧy
to found (vt)	негиздөө	negizdøø

incorporator	уюмдаштыруучу	ujumdaʃtıruutʃu
partner	өнөктөш	ønøktøʃ
stockholder	акция кармоочу	aktsija karmooʧu

millionaire	миллионер	millioner
billionaire	миллиардер	milliarder
owner, proprietor	ээси	eesi
landowner	жер ээси	ʤer eesi

client	кардар	kardar
regular client	туруктуу кардар	turuktuu kardar
buyer (customer)	сатып алуучу	satıp aluuʧu
visitor	келүүчү	kelyyʧy

professional (n)	кесипкөй	kesipkøj
expert	ишбилги	iʃbilgi
specialist	адис	adis

| banker | банкир | bankir |
| broker | далдалчы | daldalʧı |

cashier, teller	кассир	kassir
accountant	бухгалтер	buχgalter
security guard	кароолчу	karoolʧu

investor	салым кошуучу	salım koʃuuʧu
debtor	карыздар	karızdar
creditor	насыя алуучу	nasıja aluuʧu
borrower	карызга алуучу	karızga aluuʧu

| importer | импорттоочу | importtooʧu |
| exporter | экспорттоочу | eksporttooʧu |

manufacturer	өндүрүүчү	øndyryyʧy
distributor	дистрибьютор	distribjutor
middleman	ортомчу	ortomʧu

| consultant | кеңешчи | keŋeʃʧi |
| sales representative | сатуу агенти | satuu agenti |

agent	агент	agent
insurance agent	камсыздандыруучу	kamsızdandıruutʃu
	агент	agent

106. Service professions

cook	ашпозчу	aʃpoztʃu
chef (kitchen chef)	башкы ашпозчу	baʃkı aʃpoztʃu
baker	навайчы	navajtʃı

bartender	бармен	barmen
waiter	официант	ofitsiant
waitress	официант кыз	ofitsiant kız

lawyer, attorney	жактоочу	dʒaktootʃu
lawyer (legal expert)	юрист	jurist
notary public	нотариус	notarius

electrician	электрик	elektrik
plumber	сантехник	santeχnik
carpenter	жыгач уста	dʒıgatʃ usta

masseur	укалоочу	ukalootʃu
masseuse	укалоочу	ukalootʃu
doctor	доктур	doktur

taxi driver	такси айдоочу	taksi ajdootʃu
driver	айдоочу	ajdootʃu
delivery man	жеткирүүчү	dʒetkiryytʃy

chambermaid	үй кызматкери	yj kızmatkeri
security guard	кароолчу	karooltʃu
flight attendant (fem.)	стюардесса	stuardessa

schoolteacher	мугалим	mugalim
librarian	китепканачы	kitepkanatʃı
translator	котормочу	kotormotʃu

| interpreter | оозеки котормочу | oozeki kotormotʃu |
| guide | гид | gid |

hairdresser	чач тарач	tʃatʃ taratʃ
mailman	кат ташуучу	kat taʃuutʃu
salesman (store staff)	сатуучу	satuutʃu

| gardener | багбанчы | bagbantʃı |
| domestic servant | үй кызматчы | yj kızmattʃı |

| maid (female servant) | үй кызматчы аял | yj kızmattʃı ajal |
| cleaner (cleaning lady) | тазалагыч | tazalagıtʃ |

107. Military professions and ranks

private	катардагы жоокер	katardagı dʒooker
sergeant	сержант	sɑrdʒɑnt
lieutenant	лейтенант	lejtenant
captain	капитан	kapitan
major	майор	major
colonel	полковник	polkovnik
general	генерал	general
marshal	маршал	marʃal
admiral	адмирал	admiral
military (n)	аскер кызматчысы	asker kızmattʃısı
soldier	аскер	asker
officer	офицер	ofitser
commander	командир	komandir
border guard	чек арачы	tʃek aratʃı
radio operator	радист	radist
scout (searcher)	чалгынчы	tʃalgıntʃı
pioneer (sapper)	сапёр	sapⁱor
marksman	аткыч	atkıtʃ
navigator	штурман	ʃturman

108. Officials. Priests

king	король, падыша	korolⁱ, padıʃa
queen	ханыша	χanıʃa
prince	канзаада	kanzaada
princess	ханбийке	χanbijke
czar	падыша	padıʃa
czarina	ханыша	χanıʃa
president	президент	prezident
Secretary (minister)	министр	ministr
prime minister	премьер-министр	premjer-ministr
senator	сенатор	senator
diplomat	дипломат	diplomat
consul	консул	konsul
ambassador	элчи	eltʃi
counselor (diplomatic officer)	кеңешчи	keŋeʃtʃi
official, functionary (civil servant)	аткаминер	atkaminer

prefect	префект	prefekt
mayor	мэр	mer
judge	сот	sot
prosecutor	прокурор	prokuror
(e.g., district attorney)		
missionary	миссионер	missioner
monk	кечил	ketʃil
abbot	аббат	abbat
rabbi	раввин	ravvin
vizier	визирь	viziri
shah	шах	ʃaχ
sheikh	шейх	ʃejχ

109. Agricultural professions

beekeeper	балчы	baltʃı
herder, shepherd	чабан	tʃaban
agronomist	агроном	agronom
cattle breeder	малчы	maltʃı
veterinarian	мал доктуру	mal dokturu
farmer	фермер	fermer
winemaker	вино жасоочу	vino dʒasootʃu
zoologist	зоолог	zoolog
cowboy	ковбой	kovboj

110. Art professions

actor	актёр	aktior
actress	актриса	aktrisa
singer (masc.)	ырчы	ırtʃı
singer (fem.)	ырчы кыз	ırtʃı kız
dancer (masc.)	бийчи жигит	bijtʃi dʒigit
dancer (fem.)	бийчи кыз	bijtʃi kız
performer (masc.)	аткаруучу	atkaruutʃu
performer (fem.)	аткаруучу	atkaruutʃu
musician	музыкант	muzıkant
pianist	пианист	pianist
guitar player	гитарист	gitarist
conductor (orchestra ~)	дирижёр	diridʒior
composer	композитор	kompozitor

impresario	импресарио	impresario
film director	режиссёр	redʒissʲor
producer	продюсер	produser
scriptwriter	сценарист	stsenarist
critic	сынчы	sınʧı

writer	жазуучу	dʒazuuʧu
poet	акын	akın
sculptor	бедизчи	bedizʧi
artist (painter)	сүрөтчү	syrøtʧy

juggler	жонглёр	dʒonglʲor
clown	маскарапоз	maskarapoz
acrobat	акробат	akrobat
magician	көз боечу	køz boeʧu

111. Various professions

doctor	доктур	doktur
nurse	медсестра	medsestra
psychiatrist	психиатр	psiχiatr
dentist	тиш доктур	tiʃ doktur
surgeon	хирург	χirurg

astronaut	астронавт	astronavt
astronomer	астроном	astronom
pilot	учкуч	uʧkuʧ

driver (of taxi, etc.)	айдоочу	ajdooʧu
engineer (train driver)	машинист	maʃinist
mechanic	механик	meχanik

miner	кенчи	kenʧi
worker	жумушчу	dʒumuʃʧu
locksmith	слесарь	slesarʲ
joiner (carpenter)	жыгач уста	dʒɪgaʧ usta
turner (lathe operator)	токарь	tokarʲ
construction worker	куруучу	kuruuʧu
welder	ширеткич	ʃiretkiʧ

professor (title)	профессор	professor
architect	архитектор	arχitektor
historian	тарыхчы	tarıχʧı
scientist	илимпоз	ilimpoz
physicist	физик	fizik
chemist (scientist)	химик	χimik

archeologist	археолог	arχeolog
geologist	геолог	geolog
researcher (scientist)	изилдөөчү	izildøøʧy

| babysitter | бала баккыч | bala bakkıʃ |
| teacher, educator | мугалим | mugalim |

editor	редактор	redaktor
editor-in-chief	башкы редактор	baʃkı redaktor
correspondent	кабарчы	kabarʧı
typist (fem.)	машинистка	maʃinistka

designer	дизайнер	dizajner
computer expert	компьютер адиси	kompjуter adisi
programmer	программист	programmist
engineer (designer)	инженер	indʒener

sailor	деңизчи	deŋizʧi
seaman	матрос	matros
rescuer	куткаруучу	kutkaruuʧu

fireman	өрт өчүргүч	ørt øʧyrgyʧ
police officer	полиция кызматкери	politsija kızmatkeri
watchman	кароолчу	karoolʧu
detective	аңдуучу	aŋduuʧu

customs officer	бажы кызматкери	badʒı kızmatkeri
bodyguard	жан сакчы	dʒan sakʧı
prison guard	күзөтчү	kyzøtʧy
inspector	инспектор	inspektor

sportsman	спортчу	sportʧu
trainer, coach	машыктыруучу	maʃıktıruuʧu
butcher	касапчы	kasapʧı
cobbler (shoe repairer)	өтүкчү	øtykʧy
merchant	жеке соодагер	dʒeke soodager
loader (person)	жүк ташуучу	dʒyk taʃuuʧu

| fashion designer | модельер | modeljer |
| model (fem.) | модель | modelʲ |

112. Occupations. Social status

| schoolboy | окуучу | okuuʧu |
| student (college ~) | студент | student |

philosopher	философ	filosof
economist	экономист	ekonomist
inventor	ойлоп табуучу	ojlop tabuuʧu

unemployed (n)	жумушсуз	dʒumuʃsuz
retiree	баргер	baarger
spy, secret agent	тынчы	tıŋʧı
prisoner	камактагы адам	kamaktagı adam

striker	иш калтыргыч	iʃ kaltırgıtʃ
bureaucrat	бюрократ	bʉrokrat
traveler (globetrotter)	саякатчы	sajakattʃı

gay, homosexual (n)	гомосексуалист	gomoseksualist
hacker	хакер	χaker
hippie	хиппи	χippi

bandit	ууру-кески	uuru-keski
hit man, killer	жалданма киши	dʒaldanma kiʃi
	өлтүргүч	øltyrgytʃ
drug addict	баңги	baŋgi
drug dealer	баңгизат сатуучу	baŋgizat satuutʃu
prostitute (fem.)	сойку	sojku
pimp	жан бакты	dʒan baktı

sorcerer	жадыгөй	dʒadıgøj
sorceress (evil ~)	жадыгөй	dʒadıgøj
pirate	деңиз каракчысы	deŋiz karaktʃısı
slave	кул	kul
samurai	самурай	samuraj
savage (primitive)	жапайы	dʒapajı

Sports

113. Kinds of sports. Sportspersons

sportsman	спортчу	sporttʃu
kind of sports	спорттун түрү	sporttun tyry
basketball	баскетбол	basketbol
basketball player	баскетбол ойноочу	basketbol ojnootʃu
baseball	бейсбол	bejsbol
baseball player	бейсбол ойноочу	bejsbol ojnootʃu
soccer	футбол	futbol
soccer player	футбол ойноочу	futbol ojnootʃu
goalkeeper	дарбазачы	darbazatʃı
hockey	хоккей	χokkej
hockey player	хоккей ойноочу	χokkej ojnootʃu
volleyball	волейбол	volejbol
volleyball player	волейбол ойноочу	volejbol ojnootʃu
boxing	бокс	boks
boxer	бокс мушташуучу	boks muʃtaʃuutʃu
wrestling	күрөш	kyrøʃ
wrestler	күрөшчү	kyrøʃtʃy
karate	карате	karate
karate fighter	карате мушташуучу	karate muʃtaʃuutʃu
judo	дзюдо	dzʉdo
judo athlete	дзюдо чалуучу	dzʉdo tʃaluutʃu
tennis	теннис	tennis
tennis player	теннис ойноочу	tennis ojnootʃu
swimming	сүзүү	syzyy
swimmer	сүзүүчү	syzyytʃy
fencing	кылычташуу	kılıtʃtaʃuu
fencer	кылычташуучу	kılıtʃtaʃuutʃu
chess	шахмат	ʃaχmat
chess player	шахмат ойноочу	ʃaχmat ojnootʃu

alpinism	альпинизм	alʹpinizm
alpinist	альпинист	alʹpinist
running	чуркоо	tʃurkоо
runner	жөө күлүк	dʒøø kylyk
athletics	жеңил атлетика	dʒeŋil atletika
athlete	атлет	atlet
horseback riding	ат спорту	at sportu
horse rider	чабандес	tʃabandes
figure skating	муз бийи	muz biji
figure skater (masc.)	муз бийчи	muz bijtʃi
figure skater (fem.)	муз бийчи	muz bijtʃi
powerlifting	оор атлетика	oor atletika
powerlifter	оор атлет	oor atlet
car racing	авто жарыш	avto dʒarıʃ
racer (driver)	гонщик	gonʃtʃik
cycling	велоспорт	velosport
cyclist	велосипед тебүүчү	velosiped tebyytʃy
broad jump	узундукка секирүү	uzundukka sekiryy
pole vault	шырык менен секирүү	ʃırık menen sekiryy
jumper	секирүүчү	sekiryytʃy

114. Kinds of sports. Miscellaneous

football	американский футбол	amerikanskij futbol
badminton	бадминтон	badminton
biathlon	биатлон	biatlon
billiards	бильярд	biljard
bobsled	бобслей	bobslej
bodybuilding	бодибилдинг	bodibilding
water polo	суу полосу	suu polosu
handball	гандбол	gandbol
golf	гольф	golʹf
rowing, crew	калакты уруу	kalaktı uruu
scuba diving	сууга чөмүүчү	suuga tʃømyytʃy
cross-country skiing	чаңгы жарышы	tʃaŋgı dʒarıʃı
table tennis (ping-pong)	стол тенниси	stol tennisi
sailing	парус астында сызуу	parus astında sızuu
rally racing	ралли	ralli
rugby	регби	regbi

| snowboarding | сноуборд | snouboird |
| archery | жаа атуу | dʒaa atuu |

115. Gym

| barbell | штанга | ʃtanga |
| dumbbells | гантелдер | gantelder |

training machine	машыгуу машине	maʃiguu maʃine
exercise bicycle	велотренажёр	velotrenadʒʲor
treadmill	тегеретме	tegeretme

horizontal bar	көпүрө жыгач	køpyrø dʒɪgatʃ
parallel bars	брусдар	brusdar
vault (vaulting horse)	ат	at
mat (exercise ~)	мат	mat

jump rope	секиргич	sekirgitʃ
aerobics	аэробика	aerobika
yoga	йога	joga

116. Sports. Miscellaneous

Olympic Games	Олимпиада Оюндары	olimpiada ojɵndarɪ
winner	женүүчү	dʒeɳyytʃy
to be winning	женүү	dʒeɳyy
to win (vi)	утуу	utuu

| leader | топ башы | top baʃɪ |
| to lead (vi) | топ башында болуу | top baʃɪnda boluu |

first place	биринчи орун	birintʃi orun
second place	экинчи орун	ekintʃi orun
third place	үчүнчү орун	ytʃyntʃy orun

medal	медаль	medalʲ
trophy	трофей	trofej
prize cup (trophy)	кубок	kubok
prize (in game)	байге	bajge
main prize	баш байге	baʃ bajge

| record | рекорд | rekord |
| to set a record | рекорд коюу | rekord kojɵu |

final	финал	final
final (adj)	финалдык	finaldɪk
champion	чемпион	tʃempion
championship	чемпионат	tʃempionat

stadium	стадион	stadion
stand (bleachers)	трибуна	tribuna
fan, supporter	күйөрман	kyjørman
opponent, rival	каршылаш	karʃilaʃ

| start (start line) | старт | start |
| finish line | маара | maara |

| defeat | утулуу | utuluu |
| to lose (not win) | жеңилүү | dʒeŋilyy |

referee	судья	sudja
jury (judges)	калыстар	kalıstar
score	эсеп	esep
tie	теңме-тең	teŋme-teŋ
to tie (vi)	теңме-тең бүтүрүү	teŋme-teŋ bytyryy
point	упай	upaj
result (final score)	натыйжа	natıjdʒa

| period | убак | ubak |
| half-time | тыныгуу | tınıguu |

doping	допинг	doping
to penalize (vt)	жазалоо	dʒazaloo
to disqualify (vt)	дисквалификациялоо	diskvalifitsijaloo

apparatus	снаряд	snarʲad
javelin	найза	najza
shot (metal ball)	ядро	jadro
ball (snooker, etc.)	бильярд шары	biljard ʃarı

aim (target)	бута	buta
target	бута	buta
to shoot (vi)	атуу	atuu
accurate (~ shot)	таамай	taamaj

trainer, coach	машыктыруучу	maʃıktıruutʃu
to train (sb)	машыктыруу	maʃıktıruu
to train (vi)	машыгуу	maʃıguu
training	машыгуу	maʃıguu

gym	спортзал	sportzal
exercise (physical)	көнүгүү	kønygyy
warm-up (athlete ~)	дене көрүү	dene keryy

Education

117. School

school	мектеп	mektep
principal (headmaster)	мектеп директору	mektep direktoru
pupil (boy)	окуучу бала	okuutʃu bala
pupil (girl)	окуучу кыз	okuutʃu kız
schoolboy	окуучу	okuutʃu
schoolgirl	окуучу кыз	okuutʃu kız
to teach (sb)	окутуу	okutuu
to learn (language, etc.)	окуу	okuu
to learn by heart	жаттоо	dʒattoo
to learn (~ to count, etc.)	үйрөнүү	yjrønyy
to be in school	мектепке баруу	mektepke baruu
to go to school	окууга баруу	okuuga baruu
alphabet	алфавит	alfavit
subject (at school)	сабак	sabak
classroom	класс	klass
lesson	сабак	sabak
recess	танапис	tanapis
school bell	коңгуроо	konguroo
school desk	парта	parta
chalkboard	такта	takta
grade	баа	baa
good grade	жакшы баа	dʒakʃı baa
bad grade	жаман баа	dʒaman baa
to give a grade	баа коюу	baa kojʉu
mistake, error	ката	kata
to make mistakes	ката кетирүү	kata ketiryy
to correct (an error)	түзөтүү	tyzøtyy
cheat sheet	шпаргалка	ʃpargalka
homework	үй иши	yj iʃi
exercise (in education)	көнүгүү	kønygyy
to be present	катышуу	katıʃuu
to be absent	келбей калуу	kelbej kaluu
to miss school	сабактарды калтыруу	sabaktardı kaltıruu

to punish (vt)	жазалоо	dʒazaloo
punishment	жаза	dʒaza
conduct (behavior)	жүрүм-турум	dʒyrym-turum

report card	күндөлүк	kyndølyk
pencil	карандаш	karandaʃ
eraser	өчүргүч	øtʃyrgytʃ
chalk	бор	bor
pencil case	калем салгыч	kalem salgɪtʃ

schoolbag	портфель	portfelʲ
pen	калем сап	kalem sap
school notebook	дептер	depter
textbook	китеп	kitep
drafting compass	циркуль	tsɪrkulʲ

| to make technical drawings | чийүү | tʃijyy |
| technical drawing | чийме | tʃijme |

poem	ыр сап	ɪr sap
by heart (adv)	жатка	dʒatka
to learn by heart	жаттоо	dʒattoo

school vacation	эс алуу	es aluu
to be on vacation	эс алууда болуу	es aluuda boluu
to spend one's vacation	эс алууну өткөзүү	es aluunu øtkøzyy

test (written math ~)	текшерүү иш	tekʃeryy iʃ
essay (composition)	дил баян	dil bajan
dictation	жат жаздыруу	dʒat dʒazdɪruu
exam (examination)	экзамен	ekzamen
to take an exam	экзамен тапшыруу	ekzamen tapʃɪruu
experiment (e.g., chemistry ~)	тажрыйба	tadʒrɪjba

118. College. University

academy	академия	akademija
university	университет	universitet
faculty (e.g., ~ of Medicine)	факультет	fakulʲtet

student (masc.)	студент бала	student bala
student (fem.)	студент кыз	student kɪz
lecturer (teacher)	мугалим	mugalim

lecture hall, room	дарскана	darskana
graduate	окуу жайды бүтүрүүчү	okuu dʒajdɪ bytyryytʃy
diploma	диплом	diplom

dissertation	диссертация	dissertatsija
study (report)	изилдөө	izildøø
laboratory	лаборатория	laboratorija
lecture	лекция	lektsija
coursemate	курсташ	kurstaʃ
scholarship	стипендия	stipendija
academic degree	илимий даража	ilimij daradʒa

119. Sciences. Disciplines

mathematics	математика	matematika
algebra	алгебра	algebra
geometry	геометрия	geometrija
astronomy	астрономия	astronomija
biology	биология	biologija
geography	география	geografija
geology	геология	geologija
history	тарых	tarıχ
medicine	медицина	meditsina
pedagogy	педагогика	pedagogika
law	укук	ukuk
physics	физика	fizika
chemistry	химия	χimija
philosophy	философия	filosofija
psychology	психология	psiχologija

120. Writing system. Orthography

grammar	грамматика	grammatika
vocabulary	лексика	leksika
phonetics	фонетика	fonetika
noun	зат атооч	zat atootʃ
adjective	сын атооч	sın atootʃ
verb	этиш	etiʃ
adverb	тактооч	taktootʃ
pronoun	ат атооч	at atootʃ
interjection	сырдык сөз	sırdık søz
preposition	препозиция	prepozitsija
root	сөздүн уңгусу	søzdyn uŋgusu
ending	жалгоо	dʒalgoo
prefix	префикс	prefiks

| syllable | муун | muun |
| suffix | суффикс | suffiks |

| stress mark | басым | basım |
| apostrophe | апострож | apostrof |

period, dot	чекит	ʧekit
comma	үтүр	ytyr
semicolon	чекитүү үтүр	ʧekityy ytyr
colon	кош чекит	koʃ ʧekit
ellipsis	көп чекит	køp ʧekit

| question mark | суроо белгиси | suroo belgisi |
| exclamation point | илеп белгиси | ilep belgisi |

quotation marks	тырмакча	tırmakʧa
in quotation marks	тырмакчага алынган	tırmakʧaga alıngan
parenthesis	кашаа	kaʃaa
in parenthesis	кашаага алынган	kaʃaaga alıngan

hyphen	дефис	defis
dash	тире	tire
space (between words)	аралык	aralık

| letter | тамга | tamga |
| capital letter | баш тамга | baʃ tamga |

| vowel (n) | үндүү тыбыш | yndyy tıbıʃ |
| consonant (n) | үнсүз тыбыш | ynsyz tıbıʃ |

sentence	сүйлөм	syjløm
subject	сүйлөмдүн ээси	syjlømdyn eesi
predicate	баяндооч	bajandooʧ

line	сап	sap
on a new line	жаңы сап	dʒaŋı sap
paragraph	абзац	abzaʦ

word	сөз	søz
group of words	сөз айкашы	søz ajkaʃı
expression	туюнтма	tujʉntma
synonym	синоним	sinonim
antonym	антоним	antonim

rule	эреже	eredʒe
exception	чектен чыгаруу	ʧekten ʧıgaruu
correct (adj)	туура	tuura

conjugation	жактоо	dʒaktoo
declension	жөндөлүш	dʒøndølyʃ
nominal case	жөндөмө	dʒøndømø
question	суроо	suroo

| to underline (vt) | баса белгилөө | baɑa belyiluu |
| dotted line | пунктир | punktir |

121. Foreign languages

language	тил	til
foreign (adj)	чет	ʧet
foreign language	чет тил	ʧet til
to study (vt)	окуу	okuu
to learn (language, etc.)	үйрөнүү	yjrønyy

to read (vi, vt)	окуу	okuu
to speak (vi, vt)	сүйлөө	syjløø
to understand (vt)	түшүнүү	tyʃynyy
to write (vt)	жазуу	dʒazuu

fast (adv)	тез	tez
slowly (adv)	жай	dʒaj
fluently (adv)	эркин	erkin

rules	эрежелер	eredʒeler
grammar	грамматика	grammatika
vocabulary	лексика	leksika
phonetics	фонетика	fonetika

textbook	китеп	kitep
dictionary	сөздүк	søzdyk
teach-yourself book	өзү үйрөткүч	øzy yjrøtkyʧ
phrasebook	тилачар	tilaʧar

cassette, tape	кассета	kasseta
videotape	видеокассета	videokasseta
CD, compact disc	CD, компакт-диск	sidi, kompakt-disk
DVD	DVD-диск	dividi-disk

alphabet	алфавит	alfavit
to spell (vt)	эжелеп айтуу	edʒelep ajtuu
pronunciation	айтылышы	ajtılıʃı

accent	акцент	aktsent
with an accent	акцент менен	aktsent menen
without an accent	акцентсиз	aktsentsiz

| word | сөз | søz |
| meaning | маани | maani |

course (e.g., a French ~)	курстар	kurstar
to sign up	курска жазылуу	kurska dʒazıluu
teacher	окутуучу	okutuuʧu
translation (process)	которуу	kotoruu

translation (text, etc.)	котормо	kotormo
translator	котормочу	kotormoʧu
interpreter	оозеки котормочу	oozeki kotormoʧu
polyglot	полиглот	poliglot
memory	эс тутум	es tutum

122. Fairy tale characters

Santa Claus	Санта Клаус	santa klaus
Cinderella	Күлала кыз	kylala kız
mermaid	суу периси	suu perisi
Neptune	Нептун	neptun

magician, wizard	сыйкырчы	sıjkırʧı
fairy	сыйкырчы	sıjkırʧı
magic (adj)	сыйкырдуу	sıjkırduu
magic wand	сыйкырлуу таякча	sıjkırluu tajakʧa

fairy tale	жомок	dʒomok
miracle	керемет	keremet
dwarf	эргежээл	ergedʒeel
to turn into ...	...га айлануу	...ga ajlanuu

ghost	арбак	arbak
phantom	көрүнчү	kørynʧy
monster	желмогуз	dʒelmoguz
dragon	ажыдаар	adʒıdaar
giant	дөө	døø

123. Zodiac Signs

Aries	Кой	koj
Taurus	Букачар	bukaʧar
Gemini	Эгиздер	egizder
Cancer	Рак	rak
Leo	Арстан	arstan
Virgo	Суу пери	suu peri

Libra	Тараза	taraza
Scorpio	Чаян	ʧajan
Sagittarius	Жаачы	dʒaaʧı
Capricorn	Текечер	tekeʧer
Aquarius	Суу куяр	suu kujar
Pisces	Балыктар	balıktar

| character | мүнөз | mynøz |
| character traits | мүнөздүн түрү | mynøzdyn tyry |

behavior	жүрүм-турум	dʒyrym-turum
to tell fortunes	төлгө ачуу	tølgø atʃuu
fortune-teller	көз ачык	køz atʃık
horoscope	жылдыз төлгө	dʒıldız tølgø

Arts

124. Theater

theater	театр	teatr
opera	опера	opera
operetta	оперетта	operetta
ballet	балет	balet
theater poster	афиша	afiʃa
troupe	труппа	truppa
(theatrical company)		
tour	гастрольго чыгуу	gastrolʲgo ʧiguu
to be on tour	гастрольдо жүрүү	gastrolʲdo ʤyryy
to rehearse (vi, vt)	репетиция кылуу	repetiʦija kıluu
rehearsal	репетиция	repetiʦija
repertoire	репертуар	repertuar
performance	көрсөтүү	kørsøtyy
theatrical show	спектакль	spektaklʲ
play	пьеса	pjesa
ticket	билет	bilet
box office (ticket booth)	билет кассасы	bilet kassası
lobby, foyer	холл	χoll
coat check (cloakroom)	гардероб	garderob
coat check tag	номерок	nomerok
binoculars	дүрбү	dyrby
usher	текшерүүчү	tekʃeryyʧy
orchestra seats	партер	parter
balcony	балкон	balkon
dress circle	бельэтаж	beljetaʤ
box	ложа	loʤa
row	катар	katar
seat	орун	orun
audience	эл	el
spectator	көрүүчү	køryyʧy
to clap (vi, vt)	кол чабуу	kol ʧabuu
applause	кол чабуулар	kol ʧabuular
ovation	дүркүрөгөн кол	dyrkyrøgøn kol
	чабуулар	ʧabuular
stage	сахна	saχna
curtain	көшөгө	køʃøgø

| scenery | декорация | dekoratsija |
| backstage | көшөгө артында | køʃøgø artında |

scene (e.g., the last ~)	көрсөтмө	kørsøtmø
act	окуя	okuja
intermission	антракт	antrakt

125. Cinema

| actor | актёр | aktʲor |
| actress | актриса | aktrisa |

movies (industry)	кино	kino
movie	тасма	tasma
episode	серия	serija

detective movie	детектив	detektiv
action movie	салгылаш тасмасы	salgılaʃ tasması
adventure movie	укмуштуу окуялуу тасма	ukmuʃtuu okujaluu tasma
sci-fi movie	билим-жалган аралаш тасмасы	bilim-dʒalgan aralaʃ tasması
horror movie	коркутуу тасмасы	korkutuu tasması

comedy movie	күлкүлүү кино	kylkylyy kino
melodrama	ый менен кайгы аралаш	ıy menen kajgı aralaʃ
drama	драма	drama

fictional movie	көркөм тасма	kørkøm tasma
documentary	документүү тасма	dokumentyy tasma
cartoon	мультфильм	mulʲtfilʲm
silent movies	үнсүз кино	ynsyz kino

role (part)	роль	rolʲ
leading role	башкы роль	baʃkı rolʲ
to play (vi, vt)	ойноо	ojnoo

movie star	кино жылдызы	kino dʒıldızı
well-known (adj)	белгилүү	belgilyy
famous (adj)	атактуу	ataktuu
popular (adj)	даңазалуу	daŋazaluu

script (screenplay)	сценарий	stsenarij
scriptwriter	сценарист	stsenarist
movie director	режиссёр	redʒissʲor
producer	продюсер	prodʉser
assistant	ассистент	assistent
cameraman	оператор	operator
stuntman	айлагер	ajlager

double (stand-in)	кейпин кийүүчү	kejpin kijyytʃy
to shoot a movie	тасма тартуу	tasma tartuu
audition, screen test	сыноо	sınoo
shooting	тартуу	tartuu
movie crew	тартуу группасы	tartuu gruppası
movie set	тартуу аянты	tartuu ajantı
camera	кинокамера	kinokamera

movie theater	кинотеатр	kinoteatr
screen (e.g., big ~)	экран	ekran
to show a movie	тасманы көрсөтүү	tasmanı kørsøtyy

soundtrack	үн нугу	yn nugu
special effects	атайын эффектер	atajın effekter
subtitles	субтитрлер	subtitrler
credits	титрлер	titrler
translation	которуу	kotoruu

126. Painting

art	көркөм өнөр	kørkøm ønør
fine arts	көркөм чеберчилик	kørkøm tʃebertʃilik
art gallery	арт-галерея	art-galereja
art exhibition	сүрөт көргөзмөсү	syrøt kørgøzmøsy

painting (art)	живопись	dʒivopisʲ
graphic art	графика	grafika
abstract art	абстракционизм	abstraktsionizm
impressionism	импрессионизм	impressionizm

picture (painting)	сүрөт	syrøt
drawing	сүрөт	syrøt
poster	көрнөк	kørnøk

illustration (picture)	иллюстрация	illʉstratsija
miniature	миниатюра	miniatʉra
copy (of painting, etc.)	көчүрмө	køtʃyrmø
reproduction	репродукция	reproduktsija

mosaic	мозаика	mozaika
stained glass window	витраж	vitradʒ
fresco	фреска	freska
engraving	гравюра	gravʉra

bust (sculpture)	бюст	bʉst
sculpture	айкел	ajkel
statue	айкел	ajkel
plaster of Paris	гипс	gips
plaster (as adj)	гипстен	gipsten
portrait	портрет	portret

self-portrait	автопортрет	avtoportrot
landscape painting	теребел сүрөтү	terebel syrøty
still life	буюмдар сүрөтү	bujumdar syrøty
caricature	карикатура	karikatura
sketch	сомо	somo

paint	боек	boek
watercolor paint	акварель	akvarelʲ
oil (paint)	майбоёк	majbojok
pencil	карандаш	karandaʃ
India ink	тушь	tuʃ
charcoal	көмүр	kømyr

| to draw (vi, vt) | тартуу | tartuu |
| to paint (vi, vt) | боёк менен тартуу | bojok menen tartuu |

to pose (vi)	атайын туруу	atajın turuu
artist's model (masc.)	атайын туруучу	atajın turuutʃu
artist's model (fem.)	атайын туруучу	atajın turuutʃu

artist (painter)	сүрөтчү	syrøttʃy
work of art	чыгарма	tʃıgarma
masterpiece	чеберчиликтин чокусу	tʃebertʃiliktin tʃokusu
studio (artist's workroom)	устакана	ustakana

canvas (cloth)	кендир	kendir
easel	мольберт	molʲbert
palette	палитра	palitra

frame (picture ~, etc.)	алкак	alkak
restoration	калыбына келтирүү	kalıbına keltiryy
to restore (vt)	калыбына келтирүү	kalıbına keltiryy

127. Literature & Poetry

literature	адабият	adabijat
author (writer)	автор	avtor
pseudonym	лакап ат	lakap at

book	китеп	kitep
volume	том	tom
table of contents	мазмун	mazmun
page	бет	bet
main character	башкы каарман	baʃkı kaarman
autograph	кол тамга	kol tamga

short story	окуя	okuja
story (novella)	аңгеме	aŋgeme
novel	роман	roman
work (writing)	дил баян	dil bajan

fable	тамсил	tamsil
detective novel	детектив	detektiv

poem (verse)	ыр сап	ır sap
poetry	поэзия	poezija
poem (epic, ballad)	поэма	poema
poet	акын	akın

fiction	сулуулатып жазуу	suluulatıp dʒazuu
science fiction	билим-жалган аралаш	bilim-dʒalgan alaraʃ
adventures	укмуштуу окуялар	ukmuʃtuu okujalar
educational literature	билим берүү адабияты	bilim beryy adabijatı
children's literature	балдар адабияты	baldar adabijatı

128. Circus

circus	цирк	tsırk
traveling circus	цирк-шапито	tsırk-ʃapito

program	программа	programma
performance	көрсөтүү	kørsøtyy

act (circus ~)	номер	nomer
circus ring	арена	arena

pantomime (act)	пантомима	pantomima
clown	маскарапоз	maskarapoz

acrobat	акробат	akrobat
acrobatics	акробатика	akrobatika
gymnast	гимнаст	gimnast

acrobatic gymnastics	гимнастика	gimnastika
somersault	тоңкочуктап атуу	toŋkotʃuktap atuu

athlete (strongman)	атлет	atlet
tamer (e.g., lion ~)	ыкка көндүрүүчү	ıkka køndyryytʃy

rider (circus horse ~)	чабандес	tʃabandes
assistant	жардамчы	dʒardamtʃı

stunt	ыкма	ıkma
magic trick	көз боемо	køz boemo
conjurer, magician	көз боемочу	køz boemotʃu

juggler	жонглёр	dʒonglʲor
to juggle (vi, vt)	жонглёрлук кылуу	dʒonglʲorluk kıluu
animal trainer	үйрөтүүчү	yjrøtyytʃy
animal training	үйрөтүү	yjrøtyy
to train (animals)	үйрөтүү	yjrøtyy

129   Music. Pop music

music	музыка	muzıka
musician	музыкант	muzıkant
musical instrument	музыка аспабы	muzıka aspabı
to play ...	...да ойноо	...da ojnoo
guitar	гитара	gitara
violin	скрипка	skripka
cello	виолончель	violontʃelʲ
double bass	контрабас	kontrabas
harp	арфа	arfa
piano	пианино	pianino
grand piano	рояль	rojalʲ
organ	орган	organ
wind instruments	үйлө аспаптары	yjlø aspaptarı
oboe	гобой	goboj
saxophone	саксофон	saksofon
clarinet	кларнет	klarnet
flute	флейта	flejta
trumpet	сурнай	surnaj
accordion	аккордеон	akkordeon
drum	добулбас	dobulbas
duo	дуэт	duet
trio	трио	trio
quartet	квартет	kvartet
choir	хор	χor
orchestra	оркестр	orkestr
pop music	поп-музыка	pop-muzıka
rock music	рок-музыка	rok-muzıka
rock group	рок-группа	rok-gruppa
jazz	джаз	dʒaz
idol	аздек	azdek
admirer, fan	күйөрман	kyjørman
concert	концерт	kontsert
symphony	симфония	simfonija
composition	чыгарма	tʃıgarma
to compose (write)	чыгаруу	tʃıgaruu
singing (n)	ырдоо	ırdoo
song	ыр	ır
tune (melody)	обон	obon
rhythm	ыргак	ırgak
blues	блюз	blʉz

sheet music	**ноталар**	notalar
baton	**таякча**	tajakʧa
bow	**кылдуу таякча**	kılduu tajakʧa
string	**кыл**	kıl
case (e.g., guitar ~)	**куту**	kutu

Rest. Entertainment. Travel

130. Trip. Travel

tourism, travel	туризм	turizm
tourist	турист	turist
trip, voyage	саякат	sajakat
adventure	укмуштуу окуя	ukmuʃtuu okuja
trip, journey	сапар	sapar
vacation	дем алыш	dem alıʃ
to be on vacation	дем алышка чыгуу	dem alıʃka tʃıguu
rest	эс алуу	es aluu
train	поезд	poezd
by train	поезд менен	poezd menen
airplane	учак	utʃak
by airplane	учакта	utʃakta
by car	автомобилде	avtomobilde
by ship	кемеде	kemede
luggage	жүк	dʒyk
suitcase	чемодан	tʃemodan
luggage cart	араба	araba
passport	паспорт	pasport
visa	виза	viza
ticket	билет	bilet
air ticket	авиабилет	aviabilet
guidebook	жол көрсөткүч	dʒol kørsøtkytʃ
map (tourist ~)	карта	karta
area (rural ~)	жай	dʒaj
place, site	жер	dʒer
exotica (n)	экзотика	ekzotika
exotic (adj)	экзотикалуу	ekzotikaluu
amazing (adj)	ажайып	adʒajıp
group	топ	top
excursion, sightseeing tour	экскурсия	ekskursija
guide (person)	экскурсия жетекчиси	ekskursija dʒetektʃisi

131. Hotel

hotel, inn	мейманкана	mejmankana
motel	мотель	motel
three-star (~ hotel)	үч жылдыздуу	ytʃ dʒıldızduu
five-star	беш жылдыздуу	beʃ dʒıldızduu
to stay (in a hotel, etc.)	токтоо	toktoo
room	номер	nomer
single room	бир орундуу	bir orunduu
double room	эки орундуу	eki orunduu
to book a room	номерди камдык буйрутмалоо	nomerdi kamdık bujrutmaloo
half board	жарым пансион	dʒarım pansion
full board	толук пансион	toluk pansion
with bath	ваннасы менен	vannası menen
with shower	душ менен	duʃ menen
satellite television	спутник	sputnik
air-conditioner	аба желдеткич	aba dʒeldetkitʃ
towel	сүлгү	sylgy
key	ачкыч	atʃkıtʃ
administrator	администратор	administrator
chambermaid	үй кызматкери	yj kızmatkeri
porter, bellboy	жүк ташуучу	dʒyk taʃuutʃu
doorman	эшик ачуучу	eʃik atʃuutʃu
restaurant	ресторан	restoran
pub, bar	бар	bar
breakfast	таңкы тамак	taŋkı tamak
dinner	кечки тамак	ketʃki tamak
buffet	шведче стол	ʃvedtʃe stol
lobby	вестибюль	vestibylʲ
elevator	лифт	lift
DO NOT DISTURB	ТЫНЧЫБЫЗДЫ АЛБАГЫЛА!	tıntʃıbızdı albagıla!
NO SMOKING	ТАМЕКИ ЧЕГҮҮГӨ БОЛБОЙТ!	tameki tʃegyygø bolbojt!

132. Books. Reading

book	китеп	kitep
author	автор	avtor
writer	жазуучу	dʒazuutʃu

to write (~ a book)	жазуу	ʤazuu
reader	окурман	okurman
to read (vi, vt)	окуу	okuu
reading (activity)	окуу	okuu
silently (to oneself)	үн чыгарбай	yn ʧıgarbaj
aloud (adv)	үн чыгарып	yn ʧıgarıp
to publish (vt)	басып чыгаруу	basıp ʧıgaruu
publishing (process)	басып чыгаруу	basıp ʧıgaruu
publisher	басып чыгаруучу	basıp ʧıgaruuʧu
publishing house	басмакана	basmakana
to come out (be released)	жарык көрүү	ʤarık køryy
release (of a book)	чыгуу	ʧıguu
print run	нуска	nuska
bookstore	китеп дүкөнү	kitep dykøny
library	китепкана	kitepkana
story (novella)	аңгеме	aŋgeme
short story	окуя	okuja
novel	роман	roman
detective novel	детектив	detektiv
memoirs	эсте калгандары	este kalgandarı
legend	уламыш	ulamıʃ
myth	миф	mif
poetry, poems	ыр	ır
autobiography	автобиография	avtobiografija
selected works	тандалма	tandalma
science fiction	билим-жалган аралаш	bilim-ʤalgan aralaʃ
title	аталышы	atalıʃı
introduction	кириш сөз	kiriʃ søz
title page	наам барагы	naam baragı
chapter	бөлум	bølum
extract	үзүндү	yzyndy
episode	эпизод	epizod
plot (storyline)	сюжет	suʤet
contents	мазмун	mazmun
table of contents	мазмун	mazmun
main character	башкы каарман	baʃkı kaarman
volume	том	tom
cover	мукаба	mukaba
binding	мукабалоо	mukabaloo
bookmark	чөп кат	ʧøp kat
page	бет	bet

to page through	барактоо	baraktoo
margins	талаа	talaa
annotation (marginal note, etc.)	белги	belgi
footnote	эскертүү	eskertүү

text	текст	tekst
type, font	шрифт	ʃrift
misprint, typo	ката	kata

translation	котормо	kotormo
to translate (vt)	которуу	kotoruu
original (n)	түпнуска	typnuska

famous (adj)	атактуу	ataktuu
unknown (not famous)	белгисиз	belgisiz
interesting (adj)	кызыктуу	kızıktuu
bestseller	талашып сатып алынган	talaʃıp satıp alıngan

dictionary	сөздүк	sөzdyk
textbook	китеп	kitep
encyclopedia	энциклопедия	entsiklopedija

133. Hunting. Fishing

hunting	аңчылык	aŋʧılık
to hunt (vi, vt)	аңчылык кылуу	aŋʧılık kıluu
hunter	аңчы	aŋʧı

to shoot (vi)	атуу	atuu
rifle	мылтык	mıltık
bullet (shell)	ок	ok
shot (lead balls)	чачма	ʧaʧma

steel trap	капкан	kapkan
snare (for birds, etc.)	тузак	tuzak
to fall into the steel trap	капканга түшүү	kapkanga tyʃyy
to lay a steel trap	капкан коюу	kapkan kojuu

poacher	браконьер	brakonjer
game (in hunting)	илбээсин	ilbeesin
hound dog	тайган	tajgan
safari	сафари	safari
mounted animal	кеп	kep

fisherman, angler	балыкчы	balıkʧı
fishing (angling)	балык улоо	balık uloo
to fish (vi)	балык улоо	balık uloo
fishing rod	кайырмак	kajırmak

fishing line	кайырмак жиби	kajırmak dʒıbı
hook	илгич	ilgitʃ
float, bobber	калкыма	kalkıma
bait	жем	dʒem

to cast a line	кайырмак таштоо	kajırmak taʃtoo
to bite (ab. fish)	чокулоо	tʃokuloo
catch (of fish)	кармалган балык	karmalgan balık
ice-hole	муздагы оюк	muzdagı ojuk

fishing net	тор	tor
boat	кайык	kajık
to net (to fish with a net)	тор менен кармоо	tor menen karmoo
to cast[throw] the net	тор таштоо	tor taʃtoo
to haul the net in	торду чыгаруу	tordu tʃıgaruu
to fall into the net	торго түшүү	torgo tyʃyy

whaler (person)	кит уулоочу	kit uulootʃu
whaleboat	кит уулоочу кеме	kit uulootʃu keme
harpoon	гарпун	garpun

134. Games. Billiards

billiards	бильярд	biljard
billiard room, hall	бильярдкана	biljardkana
ball (snooker, etc.)	бильярд шары	biljard ʃarı

to pocket a ball	шарды киргизүү	ʃardı kirgizyy
cue	кий	kij
pocket	луза	luza

135. Games. Playing cards

diamonds	момун	momun
spades	карга	karga
hearts	кызыл ача	kızıl atʃa
clubs	чырым	tʃırım

ace	туз	tuz
king	король	korolʲ
queen	матке	matke
jack, knave	балта	balta

playing card	оюн картасы	ojun kartası
cards	карталар	kartalar
trump	көзүр	køzyr
deck of cards	колода	koloda
point	очко	otʃko

to deal (vi, vt)	таратуу	taratuu
to shuffle (cards)	аралаштыруу	aralaʃtıruu
lead, turn (n)	жүрүү	dʒyryy
cardsharp	шумпай	ʃumpaj

136. Rest. Games. Miscellaneous

to stroll (vi, vt)	сейилдөө	sejildøø
stroll (leisurely walk)	жөө сейилдөө	dʒøø sejildøø
car ride	саякат	sajakat
adventure	укмуштуу окуя	ukmuʃtuu okuja
picnic	пикник	piknik

game (chess, etc.)	оюн	ojʉn
player	оюнчу	ojʉntʃu
game (one ~ of chess)	партия	partija

collector (e.g., philatelist)	жыйнакчы	dʒıjnaktʃı
to collect (stamps, etc.)	жыйноо	dʒıjnoo
collection	жыйнак	dʒıjnak

crossword puzzle	кроссворд	krossvord
racetrack	ат майданы	at majdanı
(horse racing venue)		
disco (discotheque)	дискотека	diskoteka

| sauna | сауна | sauna |
| lottery | лотерея | lotereja |

camping trip	жөө сапар	dʒøø sapar
camp	лагерь	lagerʲ
tent (for camping)	чатыр	tʃatır
compass	компас	kompas
camper	турист	turist

to watch (movie, etc.)	көрүү	køryy
viewer	телекөрүүчү	telekøryytʃy
TV show (TV program)	теле көрсөтүү	tele kørsøtyy

137. Photography

| camera (photo) | фотоаппарат | fotoapparat |
| photo, picture | фото | foto |

photographer	сүрөтчү	syrøttʃy
photo studio	фотостудия	fotostudija
photo album	фотоальбом	fotoalʲbom
camera lens	объектив	obʰjektiv

telephoto lens	телеобъектив	teleobʰjektiv
filter	фильтр	filʲtr
lens	линза	linza

optics (high-quality ~)	оптика	optika
diaphragm (aperture)	диафрагма	diafragma
exposure time (shutter speed)	тушугуу	tuʃuguu
viewfinder	көрүнүш табуучу	kørynyʃ tabuutʃu

digital camera	санарип камерасы	sanarip kamerası
tripod	үч бут	ytʃ but
flash	жарк этүү	dʒark etyy

to photograph (vt)	сүрөткө тартуу	syrøtkø tartuu
to take pictures	тартуу	tartuu
to have one's picture taken	сүрөткө түшүү	syrøtkø tyʃyy

focus	фокус	fokus
to focus	фокусту оңдоо	fokustu oŋdoo
sharp, in focus (adj)	фокуста	fokusta
sharpness	дааналык	daanalık

contrast	контраст	kontrast
contrast (as adj)	контрасттагы	kontrasttagı

picture (photo)	сүрөт	syrøt
negative (n)	негатив	negativ
film (a roll of ~)	фотоплёнка	fotoplʲonka
frame (still)	кадр	kadr
to print (photos)	басып чыгаруу	basıp tʃıgaruu

138. Beach. Swimming

beach	суу жээги	suu dʒeegi
sand	кум	kum
deserted (beach)	ээн суу жээги	een suu dʒeegi

suntan	күнгө күйүү	kyngø kyjyy
to get a tan	күнгө кактануу	kyngø kaktanuu
tan (adj)	күнгө күйгөн	kyngø kyjgøn
sunscreen	күнгө күйүш үчүн крем	kyngø kyjyʃ ytʃyn krem

bikini	бикини	bikini
bathing suit	купальник	kupalʲnik
swim trunks	плавки	plavki

swimming pool	бассейн	bassejn
to swim (vi)	сүзүү	syzyy
shower	душ	duʃ

| to change (one's clothes) | кийим алмаштыруу | kijim almaʃtıruu |
| towel | сүлгү | sylgy |

| boat | кайык | kajık |
| motorboat | катер | kater |

water ski	суу чаңгысы	suu ʧaŋgısı
paddle boat	суу велосипеди	suu velosipedi
surfing	тактай тебүү	taktaj tebyy
surfer	тактай тебүүчү	taktaj tebyyʧy

scuba set	акваланг	akvalang
flippers (swim fins)	ласты	lastı
mask (diving ~)	маска	maska
diver	суура сүңгүү	suuga syngyy
to dive (vi)	сүңгүү	syngyy
underwater (adv)	суу астында	suu astında

beach umbrella	зонт	zont
sunbed (lounger)	шезлонг	ʃezlong
sunglasses	көз айнек	køz ajnek
air mattress	сүзүү үчүн матрас	syzyy yʧyn matras

| to play (amuse oneself) | ойноо | ojnoo |
| to go for a swim | сууга түшүү | suuga tyʃyy |

beach ball	топ	top
to inflate (vt)	үйлөө	yjløø
inflatable, air (adj)	үйлөнмө	yjlønmø

wave	толкун	tolkun
buoy (line of ~s)	буй	buj
to drown (ab. person)	чөгүү	ʧøgyy

to save, to rescue	куткаруу	kutkaruu
life vest	куткаруучу күрмө	kutkaruuʧu kyrmø
to observe, to watch	байкоо	bajkoo
lifeguard	куткаруучу	kutkaruuʧu

TECHNICAL EQUIPMENT. TRANSPORTATION

Technical equipment

139. Computer

computer	компьютер	kompjuter
notebook, laptop	ноутбук	noutbuk
to turn on	күйгүзүү	kyjgyzyy
to turn off	өчүрүү	øtʃyryy
keyboard	ариптакта	ariptakta
key	баскыч	baskıtʃ
mouse	чычкан	tʃɪtʃkan
mouse pad	килемче	kilemtʃe
button	баскыч	baskıtʃ
cursor	курсор	kursor
monitor	монитор	monitor
screen	экран	ekran
hard disk	катуу диск	katuu disk
hard disk capacity	катуу дисктин көлөмү	katuu disktin kølømy
memory	эс тутум	es tutum
random access memory	оперативдик эс тутум	operativdik es tutum
file	файл	fajl
folder	папка	papka
to open (vt)	ачуу	atʃuu
to close (vt)	жабуу	dʒabuu
to save (vt)	сактоо	saktoo
to delete (vt)	жок кылуу	dʒok kıluu
to copy (vt)	көчүрүү	køtʃyryy
to sort (vt)	иреттөө	irettøø
to transfer (copy)	өткөрүү	øtkøryy
program	программа	programma
software	программалык	programmalık
programmer	программист	programmist
to program (vt)	программалаштыруу	programmalaʃtıruu
hacker	хакер	χaker
password	сырсөз	sırsøz

| virus | вирус | virus |
| to find, to detect | издеп табуу | izdep tabuu |

| byte | байт | bajt |
| megabyte | мегабайт | megabajt |

| data | маалыматтар | maalımattar |
| database | маалымат базасы | maalımat bazası |

cable (USB, etc.)	кабель	kabelʲ
to disconnect (vt)	ажыратуу	adʒıratuu
to connect (sth to sth)	туташтыруу	tutaʃtıruu

140. Internet. E-mail

Internet	интернет	internet
browser	браузер	brauzer
search engine	издөө аспабы	izdøø aspabı
provider	провайдер	provajder

webmaster	веб-мастер	web-master
website	веб-сайт	web-sajt
webpage	веб-баракча	web-baraktʃa

| address (e-mail ~) | дарек | darek |
| address book | дарек китепчеси | darek kiteptʃesi |

mailbox	почта ящиги	potʃta jaʃtʃigi
mail	почта	potʃta
full (adj)	толуп калган	tolup kalgan

message	кабар	kabar
incoming messages	келген кабарлар	kelgen kabarlar
outgoing messages	жөнөтүлгөн кабарлар	dʒønøtylgøn kabarlar

sender	жөнөтүүчү	dʒønøtyytʃy
to send (vt)	жөнөтүү	dʒønøtyy
sending (of mail)	жөнөтүү	dʒønøtyy

| receiver | алуучу | aluutʃu |
| to receive (vt) | алуу | aluu |

| correspondence | жазышуу | dʒazıʃuu |
| to correspond (vi) | жазышуу | dʒazıʃuu |

file	файл	fajl
to download (vt)	жүктөө	dʒyktøø
to create (vt)	жаратуу	dʒaratuu
to delete (vt)	жок кылуу	dʒok kıluu
deleted (adj)	жок кылынган	dʒok kılıngan

connection (ADSL, etc.)	байланыш	bajlanıʃ
speed	ылдамдык	ıldamdık
modem	модем	modem
access	жеткирилүү	dʒetkirilyy
port (e.g., input ~)	порт	port

| connection (make a ~) | туташуу | tutaʃuu |
| to connect to … (vi) | … туташуу | … tutaʃuu |

| to select (vt) | тандоо | tandoo |
| to search (for …) | … издөө | … izdøø |

Transportation

141. Airplane

airplane	учак	uʧak
air ticket	авиабилет	aviabilet
airline	авиакомпания	aviakompanija
airport	аэропорт	aeroport
supersonic (adj)	сверхзвуковой	sverχzvukovoj
captain	кеме командири	keme komandiri
crew	экипаж	ekipadʒ
pilot	учкуч	uʧkuʧ
flight attendant (fem.)	стюардесса	stɥardessa
navigator	штурман	ʃturman
wings	канаттар	kanattar
tail	куйрук	kujruk
cockpit	кабина	kabina
engine	кыймылдаткыч	kɯjmɯldatkɯʧ
undercarriage (landing gear)	шасси	ʃassi
turbine	турбина	turbina
propeller	пропеллер	propeller
black box	кара куту	kara kutu
yoke (control column)	штурвал	ʃturval
fuel	күйүүчү май	kyjyyʧy may
safety card	коопсуздук көрсөтмөсү	koopsuzduk kørsøtmøsy
oxygen mask	кислород чүмбөтү	kislorod ʧymbøty
uniform	бир беткей кийим	bir betkey kijim
life vest	куткаруучу күрмө	kutkaruuʧu kyrmø
parachute	парашют	paraʃɥt
takeoff	учуп көтөрүлүү	uʧup køtørylyy
to take off (vi)	учуп көтөрүлүү	uʧup køtørylyy
runway	учуп чыгуу тилкеси	uʧup ʧɯguu tilkesi
visibility	көрүнүш	kørynyʃ
flight (act of flying)	учуу	uʧuu
altitude	бийиктик	bijiktik
air pocket	аба чүңкуру	aba ʧyŋkuru
seat	орун	orun
headphones	кулакчын	kulakʧın

folding tray (tray table)	буктөлмө стол	byktølmø stul
airplane window	иллюминатор	illuminator
aisle	өтмөк	øtmøk

142. Train

train	поезд	poezd
commuter train	электричка	elektritʃka
express train	бат жүрүүчү поезд	bat dʒyryytʃy poezd
diesel locomotive	тепловоз	teplovoz
steam locomotive	паровоз	parovoz

| passenger car | вагон | vagon |
| dining car | вагон-ресторан | vagon-restoran |

rails	рельсалар	relʲsalar
railroad	темир жолу	temir dʒolu
railway tie	шпала	ʃpala

platform (railway ~)	платформа	platforma
track (~ 1, 2, etc.)	жол	dʒol
semaphore	семафор	semafor
station	бекет	beket

engineer (train driver)	машинист	maʃinist
porter (of luggage)	жук ташуучу	dʒuk taʃuutʃu
car attendant	проводник	provodnik
passenger	жүргүнчү	dʒyrgyntʃy
conductor (ticket inspector)	текшерүүчү	tekʃeryytʃy

| corridor (in train) | коридор | koridor |
| emergency brake | стоп-кран | stop-kran |

compartment	купе	kupe
berth	текче	tektʃe
upper berth	үстүңкү текче	ystyŋky tektʃe
lower berth	ылдыйкы текче	ıldıjkı tektʃe
bed linen, bedding	жууркан-төшөк	dʒuurkan-tøʃøk

ticket	билет	bilet
schedule	ырааттама	ıraattama
information display	табло	tablo

to leave, to depart	жөнөө	dʒønøø
departure (of train)	жөнөө	dʒønøø
to arrive (ab. train)	келүү	kelyy
arrival	келүү	kelyy
to arrive by train	поезд менен келүү	poezd menen kelyy
to get on the train	поездге отуруу	poezdge oturuu

to get off the train	поездден түшүү	poezdden tyʃyy
train wreck	кыйроо	kijroo
to derail (vi)	рельсадан чыгып кетүү	relʲsadan ʧɯgɯp ketyy

steam locomotive	паровоз	parovoz
stoker, fireman	от жагуучу	ot ʤaguutʃu
firebox	меш	meʃ
coal	көмүр	kømyr

143. Ship

| ship | кеме | keme |
| vessel | кеме | keme |

steamship	пароход	paroχod
riverboat	теплоход	teploχod
cruise ship	лайнер	lajner
cruiser	крейсер	krejser

yacht	яхта	jaχta
tugboat	буксир	buksir
barge	баржа	barʤa
ferry	паром	parom

| sailing ship | парус | parus |
| brigantine | бригантина | brigantina |

| ice breaker | муз жаргыч кеме | muz ʤargɯʧ keme |
| submarine | суу астында жүрүүчү кеме | suu astɯnda ʤyryytʃy keme |

boat (flat-bottomed ~)	кайык	kajɯk
dinghy	шлюпка	ʃlʉpka
lifeboat	куткаруу шлюпкасы	kutkaruu ʃlʉpkasɯ
motorboat	катер	kater

captain	капитан	kapitan
seaman	матрос	matros
sailor	деңизчи	deŋizʧi
crew	экипаж	ekipaʤ

boatswain	боцман	boʦman
ship's boy	юнга	jʉnga
cook	кок	kok
ship's doctor	кеме доктуру	keme dokturu

deck	палуба	paluba
mast	мачта	maʧta
sail	парус	parus
hold	трюм	trʉm

bow (prow)	түмшүк	tumʃuk
stern	кеменин арткы бөлүгү	kemenin artkı bølygy
oar	калак	kalak
screw propeller	винт	vint

cabin	каюта	kajʉta
wardroom	кают-компания	kajʉt-kompanija
engine room	машина бөлүгү	maʃina bølygy
bridge	капитан мостиги	kapitan mostigi
radio room	радиорубка	radiorubka
wave (radio)	толкун	tolkun
logbook	кеме журналы	keme dʒurnalı

spyglass	дүрбү	dyrby
bell	коңгуроо	koŋguroo
flag	байрак	bajrak

| hawser (mooring ~) | аркан | arkan |
| knot (bowline, etc.) | түйүн | tyjyn |

| deckrails | туткуч | tutkutʃ |
| gangway | трап | trap |

| anchor | кеме казык | keme kazık |
| to weigh anchor | кеме казыкты көтөрүү | keme kazıktı køtøryy |

| to drop anchor | кеме казыкты таштоо | keme kazıktı taʃtoo |
| anchor chain | казык чынжыры | kazık tʃındʒırı |

| port (harbor) | порт | port |
| quay, wharf | причал | pritʃal |

| to berth (moor) | келип токтоо | kelip toktoo |
| to cast off | жээктен алыстоо | dʒeekten alıstoo |

| trip, voyage | саякат | sajakat |
| cruise (sea trip) | деңиз саякаты | deŋiz sajakatı |

| course (route) | курс | kurs |
| route (itinerary) | каттам | kattam |

fairway (safe water channel)	фарватер	farvater
shallows	тайыз жер	tajız dʒer
to run aground	тайыз жерге отуруу	tajız dʒerge oturuu

storm	бороон чапкын	boroon tʃapkın
signal	сигнал	signal
to sink (vi)	чөгүү	tʃøgyy
Man overboard!	Сууда адам бар!	suuda adam bar!
SOS (distress signal)	SOS	sos
ring buoy	куткаруучу тегерек	kutkaruutʃu tegerek

144. Airport

airport	аэропорт	aeroport
airplane	учак	utʃak
airline	авиакомпания	aviakompanija
air traffic controller	авиадиспетчер	aviadispetʃer
departure	учуп кетүү	utʃup ketyy
arrival	учуп келүү	utʃup kelyy
to arrive (by plane)	учуп келүү	utʃup kelyy
departure time	учуп кетүү убактысы	utʃup ketyy ubaktısı
arrival time	учуп келүү убактысы	utʃup kelyy ubaktısı
to be delayed	кармалуу	karmaluu
flight delay	учуп кетүүнүн кечигиши	utʃup ketyynyn ketʃigiʃi
information board	маалымат таблосу	maalımat tablosu
information	маалымат	maalımat
to announce (vt)	кулактандыруу	kulaktandıruu
flight (e.g., next ~)	рейс	rejs
customs	бажыкана	badʒıkana
customs officer	бажы кызматкери	badʒı kızmatkeri
customs declaration	бажы декларациясы	badʒı deklaratsijası
to fill out (vt)	толтуруу	tolturuu
to fill out the declaration	декларация толтуруу	deklaratsija tolturuu
passport control	паспорт текшерүү	pasport tekʃeryy
luggage	жүк	dʒyk
hand luggage	кол жүгү	kol dʒygy
luggage cart	араба	araba
landing	конуу	konuu
landing strip	конуу тилкеси	konuu tilkesi
to land (vi)	конуу	konuu
airstair (passenger stair)	трап	trap
check-in	катталуу	kattaluu
check-in counter	каттоо стойкасы	kattoo stojkası
to check-in (vi)	катталуу	kattaluu
boarding pass	отуруу үчүн талон	oturuu ytʃyn talon
departure gate	чыгуу	tʃıguu
transit	транзит	tranzit
to wait (vt)	күтүү	kytyy
departure lounge	күтүү залы	kutyy zalı
to see off	узатуу	uzatuu
to say goodbye	коштошуу	koʃtoʃuu

145. Bicycle. Motorcycle

bicycle	велосипед	velosiped
scooter	мотороллер	motoroller
motorcycle, bike	мотоцикл	mototsikl
to go by bicycle	велосипедде жүрүү	velosipedde dʒyryy
handlebars	руль	rulʲ
pedal	педаль	pedalʲ
brakes	тормоз	tormoz
bicycle seat (saddle)	отургуч	oturgutʃ
pump	соркыскыч	sorkıskıtʃ
luggage rack	багажник	bagadʒnik
front lamp	фонарь	fonarʲ
helmet	шлем	ʃlem
wheel	дөңгөлөк	døŋgøløk
fender	калкан	kalkan
rim	дөңгөлөктүн алкагы	døŋgøløktyn alkagı
spoke	чабак	tʃabak

Cars

146. Types of cars

automobile, car	автоунаа	avtounaa
sports car	спорттук автоунаа	sporttuk avtounaa
limousine	лимузин	limuzin
off-road vehicle	жолтандабас	dʒoltandabas
convertible (n)	кабриолет	kabriolet
minibus	микроавтобус	mikroavtobus
ambulance	тез жардам	tez dʒardam
snowplow	кар күрөөчү машина	kar kyrøøtʃy maʃina
truck	жүк ташуучу машина	dʒyk taʃuutʃu maʃina
tanker truck	бензовоз	benzovoz
van (small truck)	фургон	furgon
road tractor (trailer truck)	тягач	tʲagatʃ
trailer	чиркегич	tʃirkegitʃ
comfortable (adj)	жайлуу	dʒajluu
used (adj)	колдонулган	koldonulgan

147. Cars. Bodywork

hood	капот	kapot
fender	калкан	kalkan
roof	үстү	ysty
windshield	шамалдан тоскон айнек	ʃamaldan toskon ajnek
rear-view mirror	арткы күзгү	artkı kyzgy
windshield washer	айнек жуугуч	ajnek dʒuugutʃ
windshield wipers	щётка	ʃtʃʲotka
side window	каптал айнек	kaptal ajnek
window lift (power window)	айнек көтөргүч	ajnek køtørgytʃ
antenna	антенна	antenna
sunroof	люк	lɯk
bumper	бампер	bamper
trunk	жүк салгыч	dʒyk salgıtʃ
roof luggage rack	жүк салгыч	dʒyk salgıtʃ
door	эшик	eʃik

| door handle | кармагыч | karmagıtʃ |
| door lock | кулпу | kulpu |

license plate	номер	nomer
muffler	глушитель	gluʃitelʲ
gas tank	бензобак	benzobak
tailpipe	калдыктар түтүгү	kaldıktar tytygy

gas, accelerator	газ	gaz
pedal	педаль	pedalʲ
gas pedal	газ педали	gaz pedali

brake	тормоз	tormoz
brake pedal	тормоздун педалы	tormozdun pedalı
to brake (use the brake)	тормоз басуу	tormoz basuu
parking brake	токтомо тормозу	toktomo tormozu

clutch	илиштирүү	iliʃtiryy
clutch pedal	илиштирүү педали	iliʃtiryy pedali
clutch disc	илиштирүү диски	iliʃtiryy diski
shock absorber	амортизатор	amortizator

wheel	дөңгөлөк	døŋgøløk
spare tire	запас дөңгөлөгү	zapas døŋgøløgy
tire	покрышка	pokrıʃka
hubcap	жапкыч	dʒapkıtʃ

driving wheels	салма дөңгөлөктөр	salma døŋgøløktør
front-wheel drive (as adj)	алдыңкы дөңгөлөк салмалуу	aldıŋkı døŋgøløk salmaluu
rear-wheel drive (as adj)	арткы дөңгөлөк салмалуу	artkı døŋgøløk salmaluu
all-wheel drive (as adj)	бардык дөңгөлөк салмалуу	bardık døŋgøløk salmaluu

gearbox	бергилик куту	bergilik kutu
automatic (adj)	автоматтык	avtomattık
mechanical (adj)	механикалуу	meχanikaluu
gear shift	бергилик кутунун жылышуусу	bergilik kutunun dʒılıʃuusu

| headlight | фара | fara |
| headlights | фаралар | faralar |

low beam	жакынкы чырак	dʒakınkı tʃırak
high beam	алыскы чырак	alıskı tʃırak
brake light	стоп-сигнал	stop-signal

parking lights	габарит чырактары	gabarit tʃıraktarı
hazard lights	авария чырактары	avarija tʃıraktarı
fog lights	туманга каршы чырактар	tumanga karʃı tʃıraktar

| turn signal | бурулуш чырагы | buruluʃ tʃɪragɪ |
| back-up light | арткы чырак | artkɪ tʃɪrak |

148. Cars. Passenger compartment

car inside (interior)	салон	salon
leather (as adj)	тери	teri
velour (as adj)	велюр	velʉr
upholstery	каптоо	kaptoo

instrument (gage)	алет	alet
dashboard	алет панели	alet paneli
speedometer	спидометр	spidometr
needle (pointer)	жебе	dʒebe

odometer	эсептегич	eseptegitʃ
indicator (sensor)	көрсөткүч	kørsøtkytʃ
level	деңгээл	deŋgeel
warning light	көрсөткүч	kørsøtkytʃ

steering wheel	руль	rulʲ
horn	сигнал	signal
button	баскыч	baskɪtʃ
switch	которгуч	kotorgutʃ

seat	орун	orun
backrest	желөнгүч	dʒøløngytʃ
headrest	баш жөлөгүч	baʃ dʒøløgytʃ
seat belt	орундук куру	orunduk kuru
to fasten the belt	курду тагынуу	kurdu tagɪnuu
adjustment (of seats)	жөндөө	dʒøndøø

| airbag | аба жаздыкчасы | aba dʒazdɪktʃasɪ |
| air-conditioner | аба желдеткич | aba dʒeldetkitʃ |

radio	үналгы	ynalgɪ
CD player	CD-ойноткуч	sidi-ojnotkutʃ
to turn on	жүргүзүү	dʒyrgyzyy
antenna	антенна	antenna
glove box	колкап бөлүмү	kolkap bølymy
ashtray	күл салгыч	kyl salgɪtʃ

149. Cars. Engine

engine	кыймылдаткыч	kɪjmɪldatkɪtʃ
motor	мотор	motor
diesel (as adj)	дизель менен	dizelʲ menen
gasoline (as adj)	бензин менен	benzin menen

engine volume	илиймылдаттыгыпын көлөмү	lɑjmıldɑtkıʧın kølømy
power	кубатуулугу	kubatuulugu
horsepower	ат күчү	at kytʃy
piston	бишкек	biʃkek
cylinder	цилиндр	tsılindr
valve	сарпкапкак	sarpkapkak
injector	бүрккүч	byrkkytʃ
generator (alternator)	генератор	generator
carburetor	карбюратор	karbʉrator
motor oil	мотор майы	motor majı
radiator	радиатор	radiator
coolant	суутуучу суюктук	suutuutʃu sujʉktuk
cooling fan	желдеткич	dʒeldetkitʃ
battery (accumulator)	аккумулятор	akkumulʲator
starter	стартер	starter
ignition	от алдыруу	ot aldıruu
spark plug	от алдыруу шамы	ot aldıruu ʃamı
terminal (of battery)	клемма	klemma
positive terminal	плюс	plʉs
negative terminal	минус	minus
fuse	эриме сактагыч	erime saktagıtʃ
air filter	аба чыпкасы	aba tʃıpkası
oil filter	май чыпкасы	maj tʃıpkası
fuel filter	күйүүчү май чыпкасы	kyjyytʃy may tʃıpkası

150. Cars. Crash. Repair

car crash	авто урунушу	avto urunuʃu
traffic accident	жол кырсыгы	dʒol kırsıgı
to crash (into the wall, etc.)	урунуу	urunuu
to get smashed up	талкалануу	talkalanuu
damage	бузулуу	buzuluu
intact (unscathed)	бүтүн	bytyn
breakdown	бузулуу	buzuluu
to break down (vi)	бузулуп калуу	buzulup kaluu
towrope	сүйрөө арканы	syjrøø arkanı
puncture	тешилип калуу	teʃilip kaluu
to be flat	желин чыгаруу	dʒelin tʃıgaruu
to pump up	үйлөтүү	yjløtyy
pressure	басым	basım
to check (to examine)	текшерүү	tekʃeryy

repair	оңдоо	oŋdoo
auto repair shop	автосервис	avtoservis
spare part	белен тетик	belen tetik
part	тетик	tetik

bolt (with nut)	буроо	buroo
screw (fastener)	буралма	buralma
nut	бурама	burama
washer	эбелек	ebelek
bearing (e.g., ball ~)	мунакжаздам	munakʤazdam

tube	түтүк	tytyk
gasket (head ~)	төшөм	tøʃøm
cable, wire	зым	zɪm

jack	домкрат	domkrat
wrench	гайка ачкычы	gajka atʃkɪtʃɪ
hammer	балка	balka
pump	соркыскыч	sorkɪskɪtʃ
screwdriver	бурагыч	buragɪtʃ

| fire extinguisher | өрт өчүргүч | ørt øtʃyrgytʃ |
| warning triangle | эскертүү үчбурчтук | eskertyy ytʃburtʃtuk |

to stall (vi)	өчүп калуу	øtʃyp kaluu
stall (n)	иштебей калуу	iʃtebej kaluu
to be broken	бузулуп калуу	buzulup kaluu

to overheat (vi)	кайнап кетүү	kajnap ketyy
to be clogged up	тыгылуу	tɪgɪluu
to freeze up (pipes, etc.)	тоңуп калуу	toŋup kaluu
to burst (vi, ab. tube)	жарылып кетүү	ʤarɪlɪp ketyy

pressure	басым	basɪm
level	деңгээл	deŋgeel
slack (~ belt)	бош	boʃ

dent	кабырылуу	kabɪrɪluu
knocking noise (engine)	такылдоо	takɪldoo
crack	жарака	ʤaraka
scratch	чийилип калуу	tʃijilip kaluu

151. Cars. Road

road	жол	ʤol
highway	кан жол	kan ʤol
freeway	шоссе	ʃosse
direction (way)	багыт	bagɪt
distance	аралык	aralɪk
bridge	көпүрө	køpyrø

parking lot	унаа токтоочу жай	unaa toktootʃu dʒaj
square	аянт	ajant
interchange	баштан өйдө өткөн жол	baʃtan øjdø øtkøn dʒol
tunnel	тоннель	tonnelʲ

gas station	май куюучу станция	maj kujʉutʃu stantsija
parking lot	унаа токтоочу жай	unaa toktootʃu dʒaj
gas pump (fuel dispenser)	колонка	kolonka
auto repair shop	автосервис	avtoservis
to get gas (to fill up)	май куюу	maj kujʉu
fuel	күйүүчү май	kyjyytʃy may
jerrycan	канистра	kanistra

asphalt	асфальт	asfalʲt
road markings	салынган тамга	salıngan tamga
curb	бордюр	bordʉr
guardrail	тосмо	tosmo
ditch	арык	arık
roadside (shoulder)	жол чети	dʒol tʃeti
lamppost	чырак мамы	tʃırak mamı

to drive (a car)	айдоо	ajdoo
to turn (e.g., ~ left)	бурулуу	buruluu
to make a U-turn	артка кайтуу	artka kajtuu
reverse (~ gear)	артка айдоо	artka ajdoo

to honk (vi)	сигнал берүү	signal beryy
honk (sound)	дабыш сигналы	dabıʃ signalı
to get stuck (in the mud, etc.)	тыгылып калуу	tıgılıp kaluu
to spin the wheels	сүйрөө	syjrøø
to cut, to turn off (vt)	басаңдатуу	basaŋdatuu

speed	ылдамдык	ıldamdık
to exceed the speed limit	ылдамдыктан ашуу	ıldamdıktan aʃuu
to give a ticket	айып салуу	ajıp saluu
traffic lights	светофор	svetofor
driver's license	айдоочу күбөлүгү	ajdootʃu kybølygy

grade crossing	кесип өтмө	kesip øtmø
intersection	кесилиш	kesiliʃ
crosswalk	жөө жүрүүчүлөр жолу	dʒøø dʒyryytʃylør dʒolu
bend, curve	бурулуш	buruluʃ
pedestrian zone	жөө жүрүүчүлөр алкагы	dʒøø dʒyryytʃylør alkagı

PEOPLE. LIFE EVENTS

Life events

152. Holidays. Event

celebration, holiday	майрам	majram
national day	улуттук	uluttuk
public holiday	майрам күнү	majram kyny
to commemorate (vt)	майрамдоо	majramdoo
event (happening)	окуя	okuja
event (organized activity)	иш-чара	iʃ-ʧara
banquet (party)	банкет	banket
reception (formal party)	кабыл алуу	kabıl aluu
feast	той	toj
anniversary	жылдык	ʤıldık
jubilee	юбилей	jubilej
to celebrate (vt)	белгилөө	belgiløø
New Year	Жаны жыл	ʤanı ʤıl
Happy New Year!	Жаны Жылыңар менен!	ʤanı ʤılıŋar menen!
Santa Claus	Аяз ата, Санта Клаус	ajaz ata, santa klaus
Christmas	Рождество	roʤdestvo
Merry Christmas!	Рождество майрамыңыз менен!	roʤdestvo majramıŋız menen!
Christmas tree	Жаңы жылдык балаты	ʤaŋı ʤıldık balatı
fireworks (fireworks show)	салют	salʉt
wedding	үйлөнүү той	yjlønyy toy
groom	күйөө	kyjøø
bride	колукту	koluktu
to invite (vt)	чакыруу	ʧakıruu
invitation card	чакыруу	ʧakıruu
guest	конок	konok
to visit (~ your parents, etc.)	конокко баруу	konokko baruu
to meet the guests	конок тосуу	konok tosuu
gift, present	белек	belek
to give (sth as present)	белек берүү	belek beryy

| to receive gifts | белек алуу | bøløk aluu |
| bouquet (of flowers) | десте | deste |

| congratulations | куттуктоо | kuttuktoo |
| to congratulate (vt) | куттуктоо | kuttuktoo |

greeting card	куттуктоо ачык каты	kuttuktoo atʃık katı
to send a postcard	ачык катты жөнөтүү	atʃık kattı dʒønøtyy
to get a postcard	ачык катты алуу	atʃık kattı aluu

toast	каалоо тилек	kaaloo tilek
to offer (a drink, etc.)	ооз тийгизүү	ooz tijgizyy
champagne	шампан	ʃampan

to enjoy oneself	көңүл ачуу	køŋyl atʃuu
merriment (gaiety)	көңүлдүүлүк	køŋyldyylyk
joy (emotion)	кубаныч	kubanıtʃ

| dance | бий | bij |
| to dance (vi, vt) | бийлөө | bijløø |

| waltz | вальс | valʲs |
| tango | танго | tango |

153. Funerals. Burial

cemetery	мүрзө	myrzø
grave, tomb	мүрзө	myrzø
cross	крест	krest
gravestone	мүрзө үстүндөгү жазуу	myrzø ystyndøgy dʒazuu
fence	тосмо	tosmo
chapel	кичинекей чиркөө	kitʃinekej tʃirkøø

death	өлүм	ølym
to die (vi)	өлүү	ølyy
the deceased	маркум	markum
mourning	аза	aza

to bury (vt)	көмүү	kømyy
funeral home	ырасым бюросу	ırasım bʉrosu
funeral	сөөк узатуу жана көмүү	søøk uzatuu dʒana kømyy

wreath	гүлчамбар	gyltʃambar
casket, coffin	табыт	tabıt
hearse	катафалк	katafalk
shroud	кепин	kepin

funeral procession	узатуу жүрүшү	uzatuu dʒyryʃy
funerary urn	сөөк күлдүн кутусу	søøk kyldyn kutusu
crematory	крематорий	krematorij

obituary	некролог	nekrolog
to cry (weep)	ыйлоо	ıjloo
to sob (vi)	боздоп ыйлоо	bozdop ıjloo

154. War. Soldiers

platoon	взвод	vzvod
company	рота	rota
regiment	полк	polk
army	армия	armija
division	дивизия	divizija

| section, squad | отряд | otrʲad |
| host (army) | куралдуу аскер | kuralduu asker |

| soldier | аскер | asker |
| officer | офицер | ofitser |

private	катардагы жоокер	katardagı dʒooker
sergeant	сержант	serdʒant
lieutenant	лейтенант	lejtenant
captain	капитан	kapitan
major	майор	major
colonel	полковник	polkovnik
general	генерал	general

sailor	денизчи	deŋiztʃi
captain	капитан	kapitan
boatswain	боцман	botsman

artilleryman	артиллерист	artillerist
paratrooper	десантник	desantnik
pilot	учкуч	utʃkutʃ
navigator	штурман	ʃturman
mechanic	механик	meχanik

pioneer (sapper)	сапёр	sapʲor
parachutist	парашютист	paraʃutist
reconnaissance scout	чалгынчы	tʃalgıntʃı
sniper	көзатар	køzatar

patrol (group)	жол-күзөт	dʒol-kyzøt
to patrol (vt)	жол-күзөткө чыгуу	dʒol-kyzøtkø tʃıguu
sentry, guard	сакчы	saktʃı

warrior	жоокер	dʒooker
patriot	мекенчил	mekentʃil
hero	баатыр	baatır
heroine	баатыр айым	baatır ajım
traitor	чыккынчы	tʃıkkıntʃı

to betray (vt)	кыянаттык кылуу	kіјаnаttіk kіluu
deserter	качкын	katʃkın
to desert (vi)	качуу	katʃuu

mercenary	жалданма	dʒaldanma
recruit	жаңы алынган аскер	dʒaŋı alıngan asker
volunteer	ыктыярчы	ıktıjartʃı

dead (n)	өлтүрүлгөн	øltyrylgøn
wounded (n)	жарадар	dʒaradar
prisoner of war	туткун	tutkun

155. War. Military actions. Part 1

war	согуш	soguʃ
to be at war	согушуу	soguʃuu
civil war	жарандык согуш	dʒarandık soguʃ

treacherously (adv)	жүзү каралык менен кол салуу	dʒyzy karalık menen kol saluu
declaration of war	согушту жарыялоо	soguʃtu dʒarıjaloo
to declare (~ war)	согуш жарыялоо	soguʃ dʒarıjaloo
aggression	агрессия	agressija
to attack (invade)	кол салуу	kol saluu

to invade (vt)	басып алуу	basıp aluu
invader	баскынчы	baskıntʃı
conqueror	басып алуучу	basıp aluutʃu

defense	коргонуу	korgonuu
to defend (a country, etc.)	коргоо	korgoo
to defend (against ...)	коргонуу	korgonuu

enemy	душман	duʃman
foe, adversary	каршылаш	karʃilaʃ
enemy (as adj)	душмандын	duʃmandın

| strategy | стратегия | strategija |
| tactics | тактика | taktika |

order	буйрук	bujruk
command (order)	команда	komanda
to order (vt)	буйрук берүү	bujruk beryy
mission	тапшырма	tapʃırma
secret (adj)	жашыруун	dʒaʃiruun

battle	салгылаш	salgılaʃ
battle	согуш	soguʃ
combat	салгылаш	salgılaʃ
attack	чабуул	tʃabuul

charge (assault)	чабуул	tʃabuul
to storm (vt)	чабуул жасоо	tʃabuul dʒasoo
siege (to be under ~)	тегеректеп курчоо	tegerektep kurtʃoo

| offensive (n) | чабуул | tʃabuul |
| to go on the offensive | чабуул салуу | tʃabuul saluu |

| retreat | чегинүү | tʃeginyy |
| to retreat (vi) | чегинүү | tʃeginyy |

| encirclement | курчоо | kurtʃoo |
| to encircle (vt) | курчоого алуу | kurtʃoogo aluu |

bombing (by aircraft)	бомба жаадыруу	bomba dʒaadıruu
to drop a bomb	бомба таштоо	bomba taʃtoo
to bomb (vt)	бомба жаадыруу	bomba dʒaadıruu
explosion	жарылуу	dʒarıluu

shot	атылуу	atıluu
to fire (~ a shot)	атуу	atuu
firing (burst of ~)	атуу	atuu

to aim (to point a weapon)	мээлөө	meeløø
to point (a gun)	мээлөө	meeløø
to hit (the target)	тийүү	tijyy

to sink (~ a ship)	чөктүрүү	tʃøktyryy
hole (in a ship)	тешик	teʃik
to founder, to sink (vi)	суу астына кетүү	suu astına ketyy

front (war ~)	майдан	majdan
evacuation	эвакуация	evakuatsija
to evacuate (vt)	эвакуациялоо	evakuatsijaloo

trench	окоп	okop
barbwire	тикендүү зым	tikendyy zım
barrier (anti tank ~)	тосмо	tosmo
watchtower	мунара	munara

military hospital	госпиталь	gospitalʲ
to wound (vt)	жарадар кылуу	dʒaradar kıluu
wound	жара	dʒara
wounded (n)	жарадар	dʒaradar
to be wounded	жаракат алуу	dʒarakat aluu
serious (wound)	оор жаракат	oor dʒarakat

156. Weapons

| weapons | курал | kural |
| firearms | курал жарак | kural dʒarak |

cold weapons (knives, etc.)	атылбас курал	atılbas kural
chemical weapons	химиялык курал	ximijalık kural
nuclear (adj)	ядерлүү	jaderlyy
nuclear weapons	ядерлүү курал	jaderlyy kural
bomb	бомба	bomba
atomic bomb	атом бомбасы	atom bombası
pistol (gun)	тапанча	tapantʃa
rifle	мылтык	mıltık
submachine gun	автомат	avtomat
machine gun	пулемёт	pulemʲot
muzzle	мылтыктын оозу	mıltıktın oozu
barrel	ствол	stvol
caliber	калибр	kalibr
trigger	курок	kurok
sight (aiming device)	кароолго алуу	karoolgo aluu
magazine	магазин	magazin
butt (shoulder stock)	күндак	kyndak
hand grenade	граната	granata
explosive	жарылуучу зат	dʒarıluutʃu zat
bullet	ок	ok
cartridge	патрон	patron
charge	дүрмөк	dyrmøk
ammunition	ок-дары	ok-darı
bomber (aircraft)	бомбалоочу	bombalootʃu
fighter	кыйраткыч учак	kıjratkıtʃ utʃak
helicopter	вертолёт	vertolʲot
anti-aircraft gun	зенитка	zenitka
tank	танк	tank
tank gun	замбирек	zambirek
artillery	артиллерия	artillerija
gun (cannon, howitzer)	замбирек	zambirek
to lay (a gun)	мээлөө	meeløø
shell (projectile)	снаряд	snarʲad
mortar bomb	мина	mina
mortar	миномёт	minomʲot
splinter (shell fragment)	сыныктар	sınıktar
submarine	суу астында жүрүүчү кеме	suu astında dʒyryytʃy keme
torpedo	торпеда	torpeda
missile	ракета	raketa

161

to load (gun)	октоо	oktoo
to shoot (vi)	атуу	atuu
to point at (the cannon)	мээлөө	meeløø
bayonet	найза	najza
rapier	шпага	ʃpaga
saber (e.g., cavalry ~)	кылыч	kılıtʃ
spear (weapon)	найза	najza
bow	жаа	dʒaa
arrow	жебе	dʒebe
musket	мушкет	muʃket
crossbow	арбалет	arbalet

157. Ancient people

primitive (prehistoric)	алгачкы	algatʃkı
prehistoric (adj)	тарыхтан илгери	tarıχtan ilgeri
ancient (~ civilization)	байыркы	bajırkı
Stone Age	Таш доору	taʃ dooru
Bronze Age	Коло доору	kolo dooru
Ice Age	Муз доору	muz dooru
tribe	уруу	uruu
cannibal	адам жегич	adam dʒegitʃ
hunter	аңчы	aŋtʃı
to hunt (vi, vt)	аңчылык кылуу	aŋtʃılık kıluu
mammoth	мамонт	mamont
cave	үңкүр	yŋkyr
fire	от	ot
campfire	от	ot
cave painting	ташка чегерилген сүрөт	taʃka tʃegerilgen syrøt
tool (e.g., stone ax)	эмгек куралы	emgek kuralı
spear	найза	najza
stone ax	таш балта	taʃ balta
to be at war	согушуу	soguʃuu
to domesticate (vt)	колго көндүрүү	kolgo køndyryy
idol	бут	but
to worship (vt)	сыйынуу	sıjınuu
superstition	жок нерсеге ишенүү	dʒok nersege iʃenyy
rite	ырым-жырым	ırım-dʒırım
evolution	эволюция	evolʉtsija
development	өнүгүү	ønygyy
disappearance (extinction)	жок болуу	dʒok boluu
to adapt oneself	ылайыкташуу	ılajıktaʃuu
archeology	археология	arχeologija

| archeologist | археолог | arχeoloɡy |
| archeological (adj) | археологиялык | arχeologijalık |

excavation site	казуу жери	kazuu dʒeri
excavations	казуу иштери	kazuu iʃteri
find (object)	табылга	tabılga
fragment	фрагмент	fragment

158. Middle Ages

people (ethnic group)	эл	el
peoples	элдер	elder
tribe	уруу	uruu
tribes	уруулар	uruular

barbarians	варварлар	varvarlar
Gauls	галлдар	galldar
Goths	готтор	gottor
Slavs	славяндар	slavʲandar
Vikings	викингдер	vikingder

| Romans | римдиктер | rimdikter |
| Roman (adj) | римдик | rimdik |

Byzantines	византиялыктар	vizantijalıktar
Byzantium	Византия	vizantija
Byzantine (adj)	византиялык	vizantijalık

emperor	император	imperator
leader, chief (tribal ~)	башчы	baʃʧı
powerful (~ king)	кудуреттүү	kudurettyy
king	король, падыша	korolʲ, padıʃa
ruler (sovereign)	башкаруучу	baʃkaruuʧu

knight	рыцарь	rıtsarʲ
feudal lord	феодал	feodal
feudal (adj)	феодалдуу	feodalduu
vassal	вассал	vassal

duke	герцог	gertsog
earl	граф	graf
baron	барон	baron
bishop	епископ	episkop

armor	курал жана соот-шайман	kural dʒana soot-ʃajman
shield	калкан	kalkan
sword	кылыч	kılıʧ
visor	туулганын бет калканы	tuulganın bet kalkanı
chainmail	зоот	zoot

| Crusade | крест астындагы черүү | krest astındagı tʃeryy |
| crusader | черүүгө чыгуучу | tʃeryygø tʃıguutʃu |

territory	аймак	ajmak
to attack (invade)	кол салуу	kоl saluu
to conquer (vt)	ээ болуу	ee boluu
to occupy (invade)	басып алуу	basıp aluu

siege (to be under ~)	тегеректеп курчоо	tegerektep kurtʃoo
besieged (adj)	курчалган	kurtʃalgan
to besiege (vt)	курчоого алуу	kurtʃoogo aluu

inquisition	инквизиция	inkvizitsija
inquisitor	инквизитор	inkvizitor
torture	кыйноо	kıjnoo
cruel (adj)	ырайымсыз	ırajımsız
heretic	еретик	eretik
heresy	ересь	eresʲ

seafaring	деңизде сүзүү	deŋizde syzyy
pirate	деңиз каракчысы	deŋiz karaktʃısı
piracy	деңиз каракчылыгы	deŋiz karaktʃılıgı
boarding (attack)	абордаж	abordaʤ
loot, booty	олжо	olʤo
treasures	казына	kazına

discovery	ачылыш	atʃılıʃ
to discover (new land, etc.)	таап ачуу	taap atʃuu
expedition	экспедиция	ekspeditsija

musketeer	мушкетёр	muʃketʲor
cardinal	кардинал	kardinal
heraldry	геральдика	geralʲdika
heraldic (adj)	гералдык	geraldık

159. Leader. Chief. Authorities

king	король, падыша	korolʲ, padıʃa
queen	ханыша	χanıʃa
royal (adj)	падышалык	padıʃalık
kingdom	падышалык	padıʃalık

| prince | канзаада | kanzaada |
| princess | ханбийке | χanbijke |

president	президент	prezident
vice-president	вице-президент	vitse-prezident
senator	сенатор	senator
monarch	монарх	monarχ
ruler (sovereign)	башкаруучу	baʃkaruutʃu

dictator	диктатор	diktator
tyrant	зулум	zulum
magnate	магнат	magnat

director	директор	direktor
chief	башчы	baʃʧı
manager (director)	башкаруучу	baʃkaruuʧu
boss	шеф	ʃef
owner	кожоюн	koʤoʤʉn

leader	алдыңкы катардагы	aldıŋkı katardagı
head (~ of delegation)	башчы	baʃʧı
authorities	бийликтер	bijlikter
superiors	башчылар	baʃʧılar

governor	губернатор	gubernator
consul	консул	konsul
diplomat	дипломат	diplomat
mayor	мэр	mer
sheriff	шериф	ʃerif

emperor	император	imperator
tsar, czar	падыша	padıʃa
pharaoh	фараон	faraon
khan	хан	χan

160. Breaking the law. Criminals. Part 1

bandit	ууру-кески	uuru-keski
crime	кылмыш	kılmıʃ
criminal (person)	кылмышкер	kılmıʃker

thief	ууру	uuru
to steal (vi, vt)	уурдоо	uurdoo
stealing (larceny)	уруулук	uruuluk
theft	уурдоо	uurdoo

to kidnap (vt)	ала качуу	ala kaʧuu
kidnapping	ала качуу	ala kaʧuu
kidnapper	ала качуучу	ala kaʧuuʧu

| ransom | кутказуу акчасы | kutkazuu akʧası |
| to demand ransom | кутказуу акчага талап коюу | kutkazuu akʧaga talap kojʉu |

to rob (vt)	тоноо	tonoo
robbery	тоноо	tonoo
robber	тоноочу	tonooʧu
to extort (vt)	опузалоо	opuzaloo
extortionist	опузалоочу	opuzalooʧu

extortion	опуза	opuza
to murder, to kill	өлтүрүү	øltyryy
murder	өлтүрүү	øltyryy
murderer	киши өлтүргүч	kiʃi øltyrgytʃ

gunshot	атылуу	atıluu
to fire (~ a shot)	атуу	atuu
to shoot to death	атып салуу	atıp saluu
to shoot (vi)	атуу	atuu
shooting	атышуу	atıʃuu

incident (fight, etc.)	окуя	okuja
fight, brawl	уруш	uruʃ
Help!	Жардамга!	dʒardamga!
victim	жапа чеккен	dʒapa tʃekken
to damage (vt)	зыян келтирүү	zıjan keltiryy
damage	залал	zalal
dead body, corpse	өлүк	ølyk
grave (~ crime)	оор	oor

to attack (vt)	кол салуу	kol saluu
to beat (to hit)	уруу	uruu
to beat up	ур-токмокко алуу	ur-tokmokko aluu
to take (rob of sth)	тартып алуу	tartıp aluu
to stab to death	союп өлтүрүү	sojup øltyryy
to maim (vt)	майып кылуу	majıp kıluu
to wound (vt)	жарадар кылуу	dʒaradar kıluu

blackmail	шантаж кылуу	ʃantadʒ kıluu
to blackmail (vt)	шантаждоо	ʃantadʒdoo
blackmailer	шантажист	ʃantadʒist

protection racket	рэкет	reket
racketeer	рэкетир	reketir
gangster	гангстер	gangster
mafia, Mob	мафия	mafija

pickpocket	чөнтөк ууру	tʃøntøk uuru
burglar	бузуп алуучу ууру	buzup aluutʃu uuru
smuggling	контрабанда	kontrabanda
smuggler	контрабандачы	kontrabandatʃı

forgery	окшотуп жасоо	okʃotup dʒasoo
to forge (counterfeit)	жасалмалоо	dʒasalmaloo
fake (forged)	жасалма	dʒasalma

161.   Breaking the law. Criminals. Part 2

| rape | зордуктоо | zorduktoo |
| to rape (vt) | зордуктоо | zorduktoo |

rapist	**зордукчул**	zorduktʃul
maniac	**маньяк**	manjak
prostitute (fem.)	**сойку**	sojku
prostitution	**сойкучулук**	sojkutʃuluk
pimp	**жак бакты**	ʤak baktı
drug addict	**баңги**	baŋgi
drug dealer	**баңгизат сатуучу**	baŋgizat satuutʃu
to blow up (bomb)	**жардыруу**	ʤardıruu
explosion	**жарылуу**	ʤarıluu
to set fire	**өрттөө**	ørttøø
arsonist	**өрттөөчү**	ørttøøtʃy
terrorism	**терроризм**	terrorizm
terrorist	**террорист**	terrorist
hostage	**заложник**	zaloʤnik
to swindle (deceive)	**алдоо**	aldoo
swindle, deception	**алдамчылык**	aldamtʃılık
swindler	**алдамчы**	aldamtʃı
to bribe (vt)	**сатып алуу**	satıp aluu
bribery	**сатып алуу**	satıp aluu
bribe	**пара**	para
poison	**уу**	uu
to poison (vt)	**ууландыруу**	uulandıruu
to poison oneself	**ууулануу**	uulanuu
suicide (act)	**жанын кыюу**	ʤanın kıʤʉu
suicide (person)	**жанын кыйгыч**	ʤanın kıjgıtʃ
to threaten (vt)	**коркутуу**	korkutuu
threat	**коркунуч**	korkunutʃ
to make an attempt	**кол салуу**	kol saluu
attempt (attack)	**кол салуу**	kol saluu
to steal (a car)	**айдап кетүү**	ajdap ketyy
to hijack (a plane)	**ала качуу**	ala katʃuu
revenge	**кек**	kek
to avenge (get revenge)	**өч алуу**	øtʃ aluu
to torture (vt)	**кыйноо**	kıjnoo
torture	**кыйноо**	kıjnoo
to torment (vt)	**азапка салуу**	azapka saluu
pirate	**деңиз каракчысы**	deŋiz karaktʃısı
hooligan	**бейбаш**	bejbaʃ
armed (adj)	**куралданган**	kuraldangan

violence	зордук	zorduk
illegal (unlawful)	мыйзамдан тыш	mıjzamdan tıʃ
spying (espionage)	тыңчылык	tıŋʧılık
to spy (vi)	тыңчылык кылуу	tıŋʧılık kıluu

162. Police. Law. Part 1

justice	адилеттүү сот	adilettyy sot
court (see you in ~)	сот	sot
judge	сот	sot
jurors	сот калыстары	sot kalıstarı
jury trial	калыстар соту	sot
to judge, to try (vt)	сотко тартуу	sotko tartuu
lawyer, attorney	жактоочу	dʒaktooʧu
defendant	сот жообуна тартылган киши	sot dʒoobuna tartılgan kiʃi
dock	соттуулар отуруучу орун	sottuular oturuutʃu orun
charge	айыптоо	ajıptoo
accused	айыпталуучу	ajıptaluutʃu
sentence	өкүм	økym
to sentence (vt)	өкүм чыгаруу	økym ʧıgaruu
guilty (culprit)	күнөөкөр	kynøøkør
to punish (vt)	жазалоо	dʒazaloo
punishment	жаза	dʒaza
fine (penalty)	айып	ajıp
life imprisonment	өмүр бою	ømyr bojʉ
death penalty	өлүм жазасы	ølym dʒazası
electric chair	электр столу	elektr stolu
gallows	дарга	darga
to execute (vt)	өлүм жазасын аткаруу	ølym dʒazasın atkaruu
execution	өлүм жазасын аткаруу	ølym dʒazasın atkaruu
prison, jail	түрмө	tyrmø
cell	камера	kamera
escort (convoy)	конвой	konvoj
prison guard	түрмө сакчысы	tyrmø saktʃısı
prisoner	камактагы адам	kamaktagı adam
handcuffs	кишен	kiʃen
to handcuff (vt)	кишен кийгизүү	kiʃen kijgizyy

prison break	качуу	katʃuu
to break out (vi)	качуу	katʃuu
to disappear (vi)	жоголуп кетүү	dʒogolup ketyy
to release (from prison)	бошотуу	boʃotuu
amnesty	амнистия	amnistija

police	полиция	politsija
police officer	полиция кызматкери	politsija kızmatkeri
police station	полиция бөлүмү	politsija bølymy
billy club	резина союлчасы	rezina sojultʃası
bullhorn	керней	kernej

patrol car	жол күзөт машинасы	dʒol kyzøt maʃinası
siren	сирена	sirena
to turn on the siren	сиренаны басуу	sirenanı basuu
siren call	сиренанын боздошу	sirenanın bozdoʃu

crime scene	кылмыш болгон жер	kılmıʃ bolgon dʒer
witness	күбө	kybø
freedom	эркиндик	erkindik
accomplice	шерик	ʃerik
to flee (vi)	из жашыруу	iz dʒaʃıruu
trace (to leave a ~)	из	iz

163. Police. Law. Part 2

search (investigation)	издөө	izdøø
to look for ...	... издөө	... izdøø
suspicion	шек	ʃek
suspicious (e.g., ~ vehicle)	шектүү	ʃektyy
to stop (cause to halt)	токтотуу	toktotuu
to detain (keep in custody)	кармоо	karmoo

case (lawsuit)	иш	iʃ
investigation	териштирүү	teriʃtiryy
detective	аңдуучу	aŋduutʃu
investigator	тергөөчү	tergøøtʃy
hypothesis	жоромол	dʒoromol

motive	себеп	sebep
interrogation	сурак	surak
to interrogate (vt)	суракка алуу	surakka aluu
to question (~ neighbors, etc.)	сураштыруу	suraʃtıruu
check (identity ~)	текшерүү	tekʃeryy

round-up (raid)	тегеректөө	tegerektøø
search (~ warrant)	тинтүү	tintyy
chase (pursuit)	куу	kuu
to pursue, to chase	изине түшүү	izine tyʃyy

to track (a criminal)	изине түшүү	izine tyſyy
arrest	камак	kamak
to arrest (sb)	камакка алуу	kamakka aluu
to catch (thief, etc.)	кармоо	karmoo
capture	колго түшүрүү	kolgo tyſyryy
document	документ	dokument
proof (evidence)	далил	dalil
to prove (vt)	далилдөө	dalildøø
footprint	из	iz
fingerprints	манжанын изи	mandʒanın izi
piece of evidence	далил	dalil
alibi	алиби	alibi
innocent (not guilty)	бейкүнөө	bejkynøø
injustice	адилетсиздик	adiletsizdik
unjust, unfair (adj)	адилетсиз	adiletsiz
criminal (adj)	кылмыштуу	kılmıʃtuu
to confiscate (vt)	тартып алуу	tartıp aluu
drug (illegal substance)	баңгизат	baŋgizat
weapon, gun	курал	kural
to disarm (vt)	куралсыздандыруу	kuralsızdandıruu
to order (command)	буйрук берүү	bujruk beryy
to disappear (vi)	жоголуп кетүү	dʒogolup ketyy
law	мыйзам	mıjzam
legal, lawful (adj)	мыйзамдуу	mıjzamduu
illegal, illicit (adj)	мыйзамдан тыш	mıjzamdan tıʃ
responsibility (blame)	жоопкерчилик	dʒoopkertʃilik
responsible (adj)	жоопкерчиликтүү	dʒoopkertʃiliktyy

NATURE

The Earth. Part 1

164. Outer space

space	космос	kosmos
space (as adj)	космос	kosmos
outer space	космос мейкиндиги	kosmos mejkindigi
world	дүйнө	dyjnø
universe	аалам	aalam
galaxy	галактика	galaktika
star	жылдыз	dʒıldız
constellation	жылдыздар	dʒıldızdar
planet	планета	planeta
satellite	жолдош	dʒoldoʃ
meteorite	метеорит	meteorit
comet	комета	kometa
asteroid	астероид	asteroid
orbit	орбита	orbita
to revolve (~ around the Earth)	айлануу	ajlanuu
atmosphere	атмосфера	atmosfera
the Sun	күн	kyn
solar system	күн системасы	kyn sisteması
solar eclipse	күндүн тутулушу	kyndyn tutuluʃu
the Earth	Жер	dʒer
the Moon	Ай	aj
Mars	Марс	mars
Venus	Венера	venera
Jupiter	Юпитер	jʉpiter
Saturn	Сатурн	saturn
Mercury	Меркурий	merkurij
Uranus	Уран	uran
Neptune	Нептун	neptun
Pluto	Плутон	pluton
Milky Way	Саманчынын жолу	samantʃının dʒolu

| Great Bear (Ursa Major) | Чоӊ Жетиген | tʃoŋ dʒetigen |
| North Star | Полярдык Жылдыз | polʲardık dʒıldız |

Martian	марсианин	marsianin
extraterrestrial (n)	инопланетянин	ɪnoplanetʲunin
alien	келгин	kelgin
flying saucer	учуучу табак	utʃuutʃu tabak

spaceship	космос кемеси	kosmos kemesi
space station	орбитадагы станция	orbitadagı stantsija
blast-off	старт	start

engine	кыймылдаткыч	kıjmıldatkıtʃ
nozzle	сопло	soplo
fuel	күйүүчү май	kyjyytʃy may

cockpit, flight deck	кабина	kabina
antenna	антенна	antenna
porthole	иллюминатор	illʉminator
solar panel	күн батареясы	kyn batarejası
spacesuit	скафандр	skafandr

| weightlessness | салмаксыздык | salmaksızdık |
| oxygen | кислород | kislorod |

| docking (in space) | жалгаштыруу | dʒalgaʃtıruu |
| to dock (vi, vt) | жалгаштыруу | dʒalgaʃtıruu |

observatory	обсерватория	observatorija
telescope	телескоп	teleskop
to observe (vt)	байкоо	bajkoo
to explore (vt)	изилдөө	izildøø

165. The Earth

the Earth	Жер	dʒer
the globe (the Earth)	жер шары	dʒer ʃarı
planet	планета	planeta

atmosphere	атмосфера	atmosfera
geography	география	geografija
nature	табийгат	tabijgat

globe (table ~)	глобус	globus
map	карта	karta
atlas	атлас	atlas

Europe	Европа	evropa
Asia	Азия	azija
Africa	Африка	afrika

Australia	Австралия	avstralija
America	Америка	amerika
North America	Северная Америка	severnaja amerika
South America	Южная Америка	jʉdӡnaja amerika
Antarctica	Антарктида	antarktida
the Arctic	Арктика	arktika

166. Cardinal directions

north	түндүк	tyndyk
to the north	түндүккө	tyndykkø
in the north	түндүктө	tyndyktø
northern (adj)	түндүк	tyndyk
south	түштүк	tyʃtyk
to the south	түштүккө	tyʃtykkø
in the south	түштүктө	tyʃtyktø
southern (adj)	түштүк	tyʃtyk
west	батыш	batıʃ
to the west	батышка	batıʃka
in the west	батышта	batıʃta
western (adj)	батыш	batıʃ
east	чыгыш	ʧıgıʃ
to the east	чыгышка	ʧıgıʃka
in the east	чыгышта	ʧıgıʃta
eastern (adj)	чыгыш	ʧıgıʃ

167. Sea. Ocean

sea	деңиз	deŋiz
ocean	мухит	muχit
gulf (bay)	булуң	buluŋ
straits	кысык	kısık
land (solid ground)	жер	dӡer
continent (mainland)	материк	materik
island	арал	aral
peninsula	жарым арал	dӡarım aral
archipelago	архипелаг	arχipelag
bay, cove	булуң	buluŋ
harbor	гавань	gavanʲ
lagoon	лагуна	laguna
cape	тумшук	tumʃuk

atoll	атолл	atoll
reef	риф	rif
coral	маржан	mardʒan
coral reef	маржан рифи	mardʒan rifi

deep (adj)	терең	tereŋ
depth (deep water)	терeндик	tereŋdik
abyss	түбү жок	tyby dʒok
trench (e.g., Mariana ~)	ойдуң	ojduŋ
current (Ocean ~)	агым	agım
to surround (bathe)	курчап туруу	kurtʃap turuu

| shore | жээк | dʒeek |
| coast | жээк | dʒeek |

flow (flood tide)	суунун көтөрүлүшү	suunun køtørylyʃy
ebb (ebb tide)	суунун тартылуусу	suunun tartıluusu
shoal	тайыздык	tajızdık
bottom (~ of the sea)	суунун түбү	suunun tyby

wave	толкун	tolkun
crest (~ of a wave)	толкундун кыры	tolkundun kırı
spume (sea foam)	көбүк	købyk
storm (sea storm)	бороон чапкын	boroon tʃapkın
hurricane	бороон	boroon
tsunami	цунами	tsunami
calm (dead ~)	штиль	ʃtilʲ
quiet, calm (adj)	тынч	tıntʃ

| pole | уюл | ujʉl |
| polar (adj) | полярдык | polʲardık |

latitude	кеңдик	keŋdik
longitude	узундук	uzunduk
parallel	параллель	parallelʲ
equator	экватор	ekvator

sky	асман	asman
horizon	горизонт	gorizont
air	аба	aba

lighthouse	маяк	majak
to dive (vi)	сүңгүү	syŋgyy
to sink (ab. boat)	чөгүп кетүү	tʃøgyp ketyy
treasures	казына	kazına

168. Mountains

| mountain | тоо | too |
| mountain range | тоо тизмеги | too tizmegi |

mountain ridge	тоо кыркалары	too kirkalari
summit, top	чоку	ʧoku
peak	чоку	ʧoku
foot (~ of the mountain)	тоо этеги	too etegi
slope (mountainside)	эңкейиш	eŋkejiʃ
volcano	вулкан	vulkan
active volcano	күйүп жаткан	kyjyp dʒatkan
dormant volcano	өчүп калган вулкан	øʧyp kalgan vulkan
eruption	атырылып чыгуу	atırılıp ʧiguu
crater	кратер	krater
magma	магма	magma
lava	лава	lava
molten (~ lava)	кызыган	kızıgan
canyon	каньон	kanʲon
gorge	капчыгай	kapʧigaj
crevice	жарака	dʒaraka
abyss (chasm)	жар	dʒar
pass, col	ашуу	aʃuu
plateau	дөңсөө	døŋsøø
cliff	зоока	zooka
hill	дөбө	døbø
glacier	муз	muz
waterfall	шаркыратма	ʃarkıratma
geyser	гейзер	gejzer
lake	көл	køl
plain	түздүк	tyzdyk
landscape	теребел	terebel
echo	жаңырык	dʒaŋırık
alpinist	альпинист	alʲpinist
rock climber	скалолаз	skalolaz
to conquer (in climbing)	багындыруу	bagındıruu
climb (an easy ~)	тоонун чокусуна чыгуу	toonun ʧokusuna ʧiguu

169. Rivers

river	дарыя	darıja
spring (natural source)	булак	bulak
riverbed (river channel)	сай	saj
basin (river valley)	бассейн	bassejn
to flow into ...	... куюу	... kujuu
tributary	куйма	kujma
bank (of river)	жээк	dʒeek

current (stream)	агым	agım
downstream (adv)	агым боюнча	agım bojuntʃa
upstream (adv)	агымга каршы	agımga karʃı

inundation	ташкын	taʃkın
flooding	суу ташкыны	suu taʃkını
to overflow (vi)	дайранын ташышы	dajranın taʃıʃı
to flood (vt)	суу каптоо	suu kaptoo

| shallow (shoal) | тайыздык | tajızdık |
| rapids | босого | bosogo |

dam	тогоон	togoon
canal	канал	kanal
reservoir (artificial lake)	суу сактагыч	suu saktagıtʃ
sluice, lock	шлюз	ʃluz

water body (pond, etc.)	келме	kølmø
swamp (marshland)	саз	saz
bog, marsh	баткак	batkak
whirlpool	айлампа	ajlampa

stream (brook)	суу	suu
drinking (ab. water)	ичилчү суу	itʃiltʃy suu
fresh (~ water)	тузсуз	tuzsuz

| ice | муз | muz |
| to freeze over (ab. river, etc.) | тоңуп калуу | toŋup kaluu |

170. Forest

| forest, wood | токой | tokoj |
| forest (as adj) | токойлуу | tokojluu |

thick forest	чытырман токой	tʃıtırman tokoj
grove	токойчо	tokojtʃo
forest clearing	аянт	ajant

| thicket | бадал | badal |
| scrubland | бадал | badal |

| footpath (troddenpath) | чыйыр жол | tʃıjır dʒol |
| gully | жар | dʒar |

tree	дарак	darak
leaf	жалбырак	dʒalbırak
leaves (foliage)	жалбырак	dʒalbırak
fall of leaves	жалбырак түшүү мезгили	dʒalbırak tyʃyy mezgili

| to fall (ab. leaves) | түшүү | tyʃyy |
| top (of the tree) | чоку | tʃoku |

branch	бутак	butak
bough	бутак	butak
bud (on shrub, tree)	бүчүр	bytʃyr
needle (of pine tree)	ийне	ijne
pine cone	тобурчак	toburtʃak

tree hollow	көңдөй	køŋdøj
nest	уя	uja
burrow (animal hole)	ийин	ijin

trunk	сөңгөк	søŋgøk
root	тамыр	tamır
bark	кыртыш	kırtıʃ
moss	мох	moχ

to uproot (remove trees or tree stumps)	дүмүрүн казуу	dymyryn kazuu
to chop down	кыюу	kıjʉu
to deforest (vt)	токойду кыюу	tokojdu kıjʉu
tree stump	дүмүр	dymyr

campfire	от	ot
forest fire	өрт	ørt
to extinguish (vt)	өчүрүү	øtʃyryy

forest ranger	токойчу	tokojtʃu
protection	өсүмдүктөрдү коргоо	øsymdyktørdy korgoo
to protect (~ nature)	сактоо	saktoo
poacher	браконьер	brakonjer
steel trap	капкан	kapkan

to pick (mushrooms)	терүү	teryy
to pick (berries)	терүү	teryy
to lose one's way	адашып кетүү	adaʃıp ketyy

171. Natural resources

natural resources	жаратылыш байлыктары	dʒaratılıʃ bajlıktarı
minerals	пайдалуу кендер	pajdaluu kender
deposits	кен	ken
field (e.g., oilfield)	кендүү жер	kendyy dʒer

to mine (extract)	казуу	kazuu
mining (extraction)	казуу	kazuu
ore	кен	ken
mine (e.g., for coal)	шахта	ʃaχta

shaft (mine ~)	шахта	ʃaχta
miner	кенчи	kentʃi
gas (natural ~)	газ	gaz
gas pipeline	газопровод	gazoprovod
oil (petroleum)	мунайзат	munajzat
oil pipeline	мунайзар түтүгү	munajzar tytygy
oil well	мунайзат скважинасы	munajzat skvadʒinası
derrick (tower)	мунайзат мунарасы	munajzat munarası
tanker	танкер	tanker
sand	кум	kum
limestone	акиташ	akitaʃ
gravel	шагыл	ʃagıl
peat	торф	torf
clay	ылай	ılaj
coal	көмүр	kømyr
iron (ore)	темир	temir
gold	алтын	altın
silver	күмүш	kymyʃ
nickel	никель	nikelʲ
copper	жез	dʒez
zinc	цинк	tsınk
manganese	марганец	marganets
mercury	сымап	sımap
lead	коргошун	korgoʃun
mineral	минерал	mineral
crystal	кристалл	kristall
marble	мрамор	mramor
uranium	уран	uran

The Earth. Part 2

172. Weather

weather	аба-ырайы	aba-ırajı
weather forecast	аба-ырайы боюнча маалымат	aba-ırajı bojunt͡ʃa maalımat
temperature	температура	temperatura
thermometer	термометр	termometr
barometer	барометр	barometr
humid (adj)	нымдуу	nımduu
humidity	ным	nım
heat (extreme ~)	ысык	ısık
hot (torrid)	кыйын ысык	kıjın ısık
it's hot	ысык	ısık
it's warm	жылуу	dʒıluu
warm (moderately hot)	жылуу	dʒıluu
it's cold	суук	suuk
cold (adj)	суук	suuk
sun	күн	kyn
to shine (vi)	күн тийүү	kyn tijyy
sunny (day)	күн ачык	kyn at͡ʃık
to come up (vi)	чыгуу	t͡ʃıguu
to set (vi)	батуу	batuu
cloud	булут	bulut
cloudy (adj)	булуттуу	buluttuu
rain cloud	булут	bulut
somber (gloomy)	күн бүркөк	kyn byrkøk
rain	жамгыр	dʒamgır
it's raining	жамгыр жаап жатат	dʒamgır dʒaap dʒatat
rainy (~ day, weather)	жаандуу	dʒaanduu
to drizzle (vi)	дыбыратуу	dıbıratuu
pouring rain	нөшөрлөгөн жаан	nøʃørløgøn dʒaan
downpour	нөшөр	nøʃør
heavy (e.g., ~ rain)	катуу	katuu
puddle	көлчүк	kølt͡ʃyk
to get wet (in rain)	суу болуу	suu boluu
fog (mist)	туман	tuman

foggy	туманду	tumanduu
snow	кар	kar
it's snowing	кар жаап жатат	kar dʒaap dʒatat

173. Severe weather. Natural disasters

thunderstorm	чагылгандуу жаан	ʧagılganduu dʒaan
lightning (~ strike)	чагылган	ʧagılgan
to flash (vi)	жарк этүү	dʒark etyy

thunder	күн күркүрөө	kyn kyrkyrøø
to thunder (vi)	күн күркүрөө	kyn kyrkyrøø
it's thundering	күн күркүрөп жатат	kyn kyrkyrøp dʒatat

| hail | мөндүр | møndyr |
| it's hailing | мөндүр түшүп жатат | møndyr tyʃyp dʒatat |

| to flood (vt) | суу каптоо | suu kaptoo |
| flood, inundation | ташкын | taʃkın |

earthquake	жер титирөө	dʒer titirøø
tremor, shoke	жердин силкиниши	dʒerdin silkiniʃi
epicenter	эпицентр	epiʦentr

| eruption | атырылып чыгуу | atırılıp ʧıguu |
| lava | лава | lava |

twister	куюн	kujʉn
tornado	торнадо	tornado
typhoon	тайфун	tajfun

hurricane	бороон	boroon
storm	бороон чапкын	boroon ʧapkın
tsunami	цунами	ʦunami

cyclone	циклон	ʦıklon
bad weather	жаан-чачындуу күн	dʒaan-ʧaʧınduu kyn
fire (accident)	өрт	ørt
disaster	кыйроо	kıjroo
meteorite	метеорит	meteorit

avalanche	көчкү	køʧky
snowslide	кар көчкүсү	kar køʧkysy
blizzard	кар бороону	kar boroonu
snowstorm	бурганак	burganak

Fauna

174. Mammals. Predators

predator	жырткыч	dʒɯrtkɯtʃ
tiger	жолборс	dʒolbors
lion	арстан	arstan
wolf	карышкыр	karɯʃkɯr
fox	түлкү	tylky
jaguar	ягуар	jaguar
leopard	леопард	leopard
cheetah	гепард	gepard
black panther	пантера	pantera
puma	пума	puma
snow leopard	илбирс	ilbirs
lynx	сүлөөсүн	syløøsyn
coyote	койот	kojot
jackal	чөө	tʃøø
hyena	гиена	giena

175. Wild animals

animal	жаныбар	dʒanɯbar
beast (animal)	жапайы жаныбар	dʒapajɯ dʒanɯbar
squirrel	тыйын чычкан	tɯjɯn tʃɯtʃkan
hedgehog	кирпичечен	kirpitʃetʃen
hare	коен	koen
rabbit	коен	koen
badger	кашкулак	kaʃkulak
raccoon	енот	enot
hamster	хомяк	χomʲak
marmot	суур	suur
mole	момолой	momoloj
mouse	чычкан	tʃɯtʃkan
rat	келемиш	kelemiʃ
bat	жарганат	dʒarganat
ermine	арс чычкан	ars tʃɯtʃkan
sable	киш	kiʃ

marten	суусар	suusar
weasel	ласка	laska
mink	норка	norka
beaver	кемчет	kemɥet
otter	кундуз	kunduz
horse	жылкы	dʒɪlkɪ
moose	багыш	bagɪʃ
deer	бугу	bugu
camel	төө	tøø
bison	бизон	bizon
wisent	зубр	zubr
buffalo	буйвол	bujvol
zebra	зебра	zebra
antelope	антилопа	antilopa
roe deer	элик	elik
fallow deer	лань	lanʲ
chamois	жейрен	dʒejren
wild boar	каман	kaman
whale	кит	kit
seal	тюлень	tʉlenʲ
walrus	морж	mordʒ
fur seal	деңиз мышыгы	deŋiz mɪʃɪgɪ
dolphin	дельфин	delʲfin
bear	аюу	ajʉu
polar bear	ак аюу	ak ajʉu
panda	панда	panda
monkey	маймыл	majmɪl
chimpanzee	шимпанзе	ʃimpanze
orangutan	орангутанг	orangutang
gorilla	горилла	gorilla
macaque	макака	makaka
gibbon	гиббон	gibbon
elephant	пил	pil
rhinoceros	керик	kerik
giraffe	жираф	dʒiraf
hippopotamus	бегемот	begemot
kangaroo	кенгуру	kenguru
koala (bear)	коала	koala
mongoose	мангуст	mangust
chinchilla	шиншилла	ʃinʃilla
skunk	скунс	skuns
porcupine	чүткөр	tʃʉtkør

176. Domestic animals

cat	ургаачы мышык	urgaatʃı mıʃik
tomcat	эркек мышык	erkek mıʃik
dog	ит	it
horse	жылкы	dʒılkı
stallion (male horse)	айгыр	ajgır
mare	бээ	bee
cow	уй	uj
bull	бука	buka
ox	егуз	øgyz
sheep (ewe)	кой	koj
ram	кочкор	kotʃkor
goat	эчки	etʃki
billy goat, he-goat	теке	teke
donkey	эшек	eʃek
mule	качыр	katʃır
pig, hog	чочко	tʃotʃko
piglet	торопой	toropoj
rabbit	коен	koen
hen (chicken)	тоок	took
rooster	короз	koroz
duck	ердек	ørdøk
drake	эркек ердек	erkek ørdøk
goose	каз	kaz
tom turkey, gobbler	курп	kyrp
turkey (hen)	ургаачы курп	urgaatʃı kyrp
domestic animals	уй жаныбарлары	yj dʒanıbarları
tame (e.g., ~ hamster)	колго уйретулген	kolgo yjrøtylgøn
to tame (vt)	колго уйретуу	kolgo yjrøtyy
to breed (vt)	естуруу	østyryy
farm	ферма	ferma
poultry	уй канаттулары	yj kanattuları
cattle	мал	mal
herd (cattle)	бада	bada
stable	аткана	atkana
pigpen	чочкокана	tʃotʃkokana
cowshed	уйкана	ujkana
rabbit hutch	коенкана	koenkana
hen house	тоокана	tookana

177. Dogs. Dog breeds

dog	ит	it
sheepdog	овчарка	ovtʃarka
German shepherd	немис овчаркасы	nemis ovtʃarkası
poodle	пудель	pudelʲ
dachshund	такса	taksa
bulldog	бульдог	bulʲdog
boxer	боксёр	boksʲor
mastiff	мастиф	mastif
Rottweiler	ротвейлер	rotvejler
Doberman	доберман	doberman
basset	бассет	basset
bobtail	бобтейл	bobtejl
Dalmatian	далматинец	dalmatinets
cocker spaniel	кокер-спаниэль	koker-spanielʲ
Newfoundland	ньюфаундленд	njɵfaundlend
Saint Bernard	сенбернар	senbernar
husky	хаски	χaski
Chow Chow	чау-чау	tʃau-tʃau
spitz	шпиц	ʃpits
pug	мопс	mops

178. Sounds made by animals

barking (n)	үрүү	yryy
to bark (vi)	үрүү	yryy
to meow (vi)	миёлоо	mijoloo
to purr (vi)	мырылдоо	mırıldoo
to moo (vi)	маароо	maaroo
to bellow (bull)	өкүрүү	økyryy
to growl (vi)	ырылдоо	ırıldoo
howl (n)	уулуу	uuluu
to howl (vi)	уулуу	uuluu
to whine (vi)	кыңшылоо	kıŋʃiloo
to bleat (sheep)	маароо	maaroo
to oink, to grunt (pig)	коркулдоо	korkuldoo
to squeal (vi)	чаңыруу	tʃaŋıruu
to croak (vi)	чардоо	tʃardoo
to buzz (insect)	зыңылдоо	zıŋıldoo
to chirp (crickets, grasshopper)	чырылдоо	tʃırıldoo

179. Birds

bird	куш	kuʃ
pigeon	көгүчкөн	køgytʃkøn
sparrow	таранчы	tarantʃı
tit (great tit)	синица	sinitsa
magpie	сагызган	sagızgan
raven	кузгун	kuzgun
crow	карга	karga
jackdaw	таан	taan
rook	чаркарга	tʃarkarga
duck	өрдөк	ørdøk
goose	каз	kaz
pheasant	кыргоол	kırgool
eagle	бүркүт	byrkyt
hawk	ителги	itelgi
falcon	шумкар	ʃumkar
vulture	жору	dʒoru
condor (Andean ~)	кондор	kondor
swan	аккуу	akkuu
crane	турна	turna
stork	илегилек	ilegilek
parrot	тотукуш	totukuʃ
hummingbird	колибри	kolibri
peacock	тоос	toos
ostrich	төө куш	tøø kuʃ
heron	көк кытан	køk kıtan
flamingo	фламинго	flamingo
pelican	биргазан	birgazan
nightingale	булбул	bulbul
swallow	чабалекей	tʃabalekej
thrush	таркылдак	tarkıldak
song thrush	сайрагыч таркылдак	sajragıtʃ tarkıldak
blackbird	кара таңдай таркылдак	kara taŋdaj tarkıldak
swift	кардыгач	kardıgatʃ
lark	торгой	torgoj
quail	бөдөнө	bødønø
woodpecker	тоңкулдак	toŋkuldak
cuckoo	күкүк	kykyk
owl	мыкый үкү	mıkıj yky
eagle owl	үкү	yky

wood grouse	керең кур	kereŋ kur
black grouse	кара кур	kara kur
partridge	кекилик	kekilik
starling	чыйырчык	ʧïjïrʧïk
canary	канарейка	kanarejka
hazel grouse	токой чили	tokoj ʧili
chaffinch	зяблик	zʲablik
bullfinch	снегирь	snegirʲ
seagull	ак чардак	ak ʧardak
albatross	альбатрос	alʲbatros
penguin	пингвин	pingvin

180.   Birds. Singing and sounds

to sing (vi)	сайроо	sajroo
to call (animal, bird)	кыйкыруу	kïjkïruu
to crow (rooster)	күкирикү деп кыйкыруу	kykiriky' dep kïjkïruu
cock-a-doodle-doo	күкирикү	kykiriky
to cluck (hen)	какылдоо	kakïldoo
to caw (crow call)	каркылдоо	karkïldoo
to quack (duck call)	бакылдоо	bakïldoo
to cheep (vi)	чыйылдоо	ʧïjïldoo
to chirp, to twitter	чырылдоо	ʧïrïldoo

181.   Fish. Marine animals

bream	лещ	leʃʧ
carp	карп	karp
perch	окунь	okunʲ
catfish	жаян	dʒajan
pike	чортон	ʧorton
salmon	лосось	lososʲ
sturgeon	осётр	osʲotr
herring	сельдь	selʲdʲ
Atlantic salmon	сёмга	sʲomga
mackerel	скумбрия	skumbrija
flatfish	камбала	kambala
zander, pike perch	судак	sudak
cod	треска	treska
tuna	тунец	tunets
trout	форель	forelʲ

eel	угорь	ugorʲ
electric ray	скат	skat
moray eel	мурена	murena
piranha	пиранья	piranja

shark	акула	akula
dolphin	дельфин	delʲfin
whale	кит	kit

crab	краб	krab
jellyfish	медуза	meduza
octopus	сегиз бут	segiz but

starfish	деңиз жылдызы	deŋiz dʒɪldɪzɪ
sea urchin	деңиз кирписи	deŋiz kirpisi
seahorse	деңиз тайы	deŋiz tajɪ

oyster	устрица	ustritsa
shrimp	креветка	krevetka
lobster	омар	omar
spiny lobster	лангуст	langust

182. Amphibians. Reptiles

| snake | жылан | dʒɪlan |
| venomous (snake) | уулуу | uuluu |

| viper | кара чаар жылан | kara tʃaar dʒɪlan |
| cobra | кобра | kobra |

| python | питон | piton |
| boa | удав | udav |

grass snake	сары жылан	sarɪ dʒɪlan
rattle snake	шакылдак жылан	ʃakɪldak dʒɪlan
anaconda	анаконда	anakonda

lizard	кескелдирик	keskeldirik
iguana	игуана	iguana
monitor lizard	эчкемер	etʃkemer
salamander	саламандра	salamandra

| chameleon | хамелеон | xameleon |
| scorpion | чаян | tʃajan |

| turtle | ташбака | taʃbaka |
| frog | бака | baka |

| toad | курбака | kurbaka |
| crocodile | крокодил | krokodil |

183. Insects

insect, bug	курт-кумурска	kurt-kumurska
butterfly	көпөлөк	køpøløk
ant	кумурска	kumurska
fly	чымын	tʃımın
mosquito	чиркей	tʃirkej
beetle	коңуз	koŋuz
wasp	аары	aarı
bee	бал аары	bal aarı
bumblebee	жапан аары	dʒapan aarı
gadfly (botfly)	көгөөн	køgøøn
spider	жөргөмүш	dʒørgømyʃ
spiderweb	желе	dʒele
dragonfly	ийнелик	ijnelik
grasshopper	чегиртке	tʃegirtke
moth (night butterfly)	көпөлөк	køpøløk
cockroach	таракан	tarakan
tick	кене	kene
flea	бүргө	byrgø
midge	майда чымын	majda tʃımın
locust	чегиртке	tʃegirtke
snail	үлүл	ylyl
cricket	кара чегиртке	kara tʃegirtke
lightning bug	жалтырак коңуз	dʒaltırak koŋuz
ladybug	айланкөчөк	ajlankøtʃøk
cockchafer	саратан коңуз	saratan koŋuz
leech	сүлүк	sylyk
caterpillar	каз таман	kaz taman
earthworm	жер курту	dʒer kurtu
larva	курт	kurt

184. Animals. Body parts

beak	тумшук	tumʃuk
wings	канаттар	kanattar
foot (of bird)	чеңгел	tʃeŋgel
feathers (plumage)	куштун жүнү	kuʃtun dʒyny
feather	канат	kanat
crest	көкүлчө	køkyltʃø
gills	бакалоор	bakaloor
spawn	балык уругу	balık urugu

larva	курт	kurt
fin	сүзгүч	syzgytʃ
scales (of fish, reptile)	кабырчык	kabırtʃık
fang (canine)	азуу тиш	azuu tiʃ
paw (e.g., cat's ~)	таман	taman
muzzle (snout)	тумшук	tumʃuk
maw (mouth)	ооз	ooz
tail	куйрук	kujruk
whiskers	мурут	murut
hoof	туяк	tujak
horn	мүйүз	myjyz
carapace	калканч	kalkantʃ
shell (of mollusk)	үлүл кабыгы	ylyl kabıgı
eggshell	кабык	kabık
animal's hair (pelage)	жүн	dʒyn
pelt (hide)	тери	teri

185. Animals. Habitats

habitat	жашоо чөйрөсү	dʒaʃoo tʃøjrøsy
migration	миграция	migratsija
mountain	тоо	too
reef	риф	rif
cliff	зоока	zooka
forest	токой	tokoj
jungle	джунгли	dʒungli
savanna	саванна	savanna
tundra	тундра	tundra
steppe	талаа	talaa
desert	чөл	tʃøl
oasis	оазис	oazis
sea	деңиз	deŋiz
lake	көл	køl
ocean	мухит	muχit
swamp (marshland)	саз	saz
freshwater (adj)	тузсуз суулу көл	tuzsuz suulu køl
pond	жасалма көлмө	dʒasalma kølmø
river	дарыя	darıja
den (bear's ~)	ийин	ijin
nest	уя	uja

tree hollow	көңдөй	køŋdøj
burrow (animal hole)	ийин	ijin
anthill	кумурска уюгу	kumurska ujᵤgu

Flora

186. Trees

tree	дарак	darak
deciduous (adj)	жалбырактуу	dʒalbɨraktuu
coniferous (adj)	ийне жалбырактуулар	ijne dʒalbɨraktuular
evergreen (adj)	дайым жашыл	dajɨm dʒaʃɨl

apple tree	алма бак	alma bak
pear tree	алмурут бак	almurut bak
sweet cherry tree	гилас	gilas
sour cherry tree	алча	altʃa
plum tree	кара өрүк	kara øryk

birch	ак кайың	ak kajɨŋ
oak	эмен	emen
linden tree	жөкө дарак	dʒøkø darak
aspen	бай терек	baj terek
maple	клён	klʲon

spruce	кара карагай	kara karagaj
pine	карагай	karagaj
larch	лиственница	listvennitsa
fir tree	пихта	piχta
cedar	кедр	kedr

poplar	терек	terek
rowan	четин	tʃetin
willow	мажүрүм тал	madʒyrym tal
alder	ольха	olʲχa

| beech | бук | buk |
| elm | кара жыгач | kara dʒɨgatʃ |

| ash (tree) | ясень | jasenʲ |
| chestnut | каштан | kaʃtan |

magnolia	магнолия	magnolija
palm tree	пальма	palʲma
cypress	кипарис	kiparis

mangrove	мангро дарагы	mangro daragɨ
baobab	баобаб	baobab
eucalyptus	эвкалипт	evkalipt
sequoia	секвойя	sekvoja

187. Shrubs

bush	бадал	badal
shrub	бадал	badal
grapevine	жүзүм	dʒyzym
vineyard	жүзүмдүк	dʒyzymdyk
raspberry bush	дан куурай	dan kuuraj
blackcurrant bush	кара карагат	kara karagat
redcurrant bush	кызыл карагат	kızıl karagat
gooseberry bush	крыжовник	krıdʒovnik
acacia	акация	akatsija
barberry	бөрү карагат	børy karagat
jasmine	жасмин	dʒasmin
juniper	кара арча	kara artʃa
rosebush	роза бадалы	roza badalı
dog rose	ит мурун	it murun

188. Mushrooms

mushroom	козу карын	kozu karın
edible mushroom	желе турган козу карын	dʒele turgan kozu karın
poisonous mushroom	уулуу козу карын	uuluu kozu karın
cap (of mushroom)	козу карындын телпеги	kozu karındın telpegi
stipe (of mushroom)	аякчасы	ajaktʃası
cep (Boletus edulis)	ак козу карын	ak kozu karın
orange-cap boletus	подосиновик	podosinovik
birch bolete	подберёзовик	podberiozovik
chanterelle	лисичка	lisitʃka
russula	сыроежка	sıroedʒka
morel	сморчок	smortʃok
fly agaric	мухомор	muχomor
death cap	поганка	poganka

189. Fruits. Berries

fruit	мөмө-жемиш	mømø-dʒemiʃ
fruits	мөмө-жемиш	mømø-dʒemiʃ
apple	алма	alma
pear	алмурут	almurut
plum	кара өрүк	kara øryk

strawberry (garden ~)	кулпунай	kulpunaj
sour cherry	алча	altʃa
sweet cherry	гилас	gilas
grape	жүзүм	dʒyzym

raspberry	дан куурай	dan kuuraj
blackcurrant	кара карагат	kara karagat
redcurrant	кызыл карагат	kızıl karagat
gooseberry	крыжовник	krıdʒovnik
cranberry	клюква	klʉkva

orange	апельсин	apelʲsin
mandarin	мандарин	mandarin
pineapple	ананас	ananas
banana	банан	banan
date	курма	kurma

lemon	лимон	limon
apricot	өрүк	øryk
peach	шабдаалы	ʃabdaalı
kiwi	киви	kivi
grapefruit	грейпфрут	grejpfrut

berry	жер жемиш	dʒer dʒemiʃ
berries	жер жемиштер	dʒer dʒemiʃter
cowberry	брусника	brusnika
wild strawberry	кызылгат	kızılgat
bilberry	кара моюл	kara mojʉl

190. Flowers. Plants

| flower | гүл | gyl |
| bouquet (of flowers) | десте | deste |

rose (flower)	роза	roza
tulip	жоогазын	dʒoogazın
carnation	гвоздика	gvozdika
gladiolus	гладиолус	gladiolus

cornflower	ботокөз	botokøz
harebell	коңгуроо гүл	koŋguroo gyl
dandelion	каакым-кукум	kaakım-kukum
camomile	ромашка	romaʃka

aloe	алоэ	aloe
cactus	кактус	kaktus
rubber plant, ficus	фикус	fikus

| lily | лилия | lilija |
| geranium | герань | geranʲ |

hyacinth	гиацинт	giatsint
mimosa	мимоза	mimoza
narcissus	нарцисс	nartsiss
nasturtium	настурция	nasturtsiia
orchid	орхидея	orxideja
peony	пион	pion
violet	бинапша	binapʃa
pansy	алагүл	alagyl
forget-me-not	незабудка	nezabudka
daisy	маргаритка	margaritka
poppy	кызгалдак	kızgaldak
hemp	наша	naʃa
mint	жалбыз	dʒalbız
lily of the valley	ландыш	landıʃ
snowdrop	байчечекей	bajtʃetʃekej
nettle	чалкан	tʃalkan
sorrel	ат кулак	at kulak
water lily	чөмүч баш	tʃømytʃ baʃ
fern	папоротник	paporotnik
lichen	лишайник	liʃajnik
conservatory (greenhouse)	күнөскана	kynøskana
lawn	газон	gazon
flowerbed	клумба	klumba
plant	өсүмдүк	øsymdyk
grass	чөп	tʃøp
blade of grass	бир тал чөп	bir tal tʃøp
leaf	жалбырак	dʒalbırak
petal	гүлдүн желекчеси	gyldyn dʒelektʃesi
stem	сабак	sabak
tuber	жемиш тамыр	dʒemiʃ tamır
young plant (shoot)	өсмө	øsmø
thorn	тикен	tiken
to blossom (vi)	гүлдөө	gyldøø
to fade, to wither	соолуу	sooluu
smell (odor)	жыт	dʒıt
to cut (flowers)	кесүү	kesyy
to pick (a flower)	үзүү	yzyy

191. Cereals, grains

grain	дан	dan
cereal crops	дан эгиндери	dan eginderi

ear (of barley, etc.)	машак	majak
wheat	буудай	buudaj
rye	кара буудай	kara buudaj
oats	сулу	sulu
millet	таруу	taruu
barley	арпа	arpa

corn	жүгөрү	dʒygøry
rice	күрүч	kyrytʃ
buckwheat	гречиха	gretʃiχa

pea plant	нокот	nokot
kidney bean	төө буурчак	tøø buurtʃak
soy	соя	soja
lentil	жасмык	dʒasmık
beans (pulse crops)	буурчак	buurtʃak

REGIONAL GEOGRAPHY

Countries. Nationalities

192. Politics. Government. Part 1

politics	саясат	sajasat
political (adj)	саясий	sajasij
politician	саясатчы	sajasatʃı
state (country)	мамлекет	mamleket
citizen	жаран	dʒaran
citizenship	жарандык	dʒarandık
national emblem	улуттук герб	uluttuk gerb
national anthem	мамлекеттик гимн	mamlekettik gimn
government	өкмөт	økmøt
head of state	мамлекет башчысы	mamleket baʃʧısı
parliament	парламент	parlament
party	партия	partija
capitalism	капитализм	kapitalizm
capitalist (adj)	капиталистик	kapitalistik
socialism	социализм	sotsializm
socialist (adj)	социалистик	sotsialistik
communism	коммунизм	kommunizm
communist (adj)	коммунистик	kommunistik
communist (n)	коммунист	kommunist
democracy	демократия	demokratija
democrat	демократ	demokrat
democratic (adj)	демократиялык	demokratijalık
Democratic party	демократиялык партия	demokratijalık partija
liberal (n)	либерал	liberal
liberal (adj)	либералдык	liberaldık
conservative (n)	консерватор	konservator
conservative (adj)	консервативдик	konservativdik
republic (n)	республика	respublika
republican (n)	республикачы	respublikaʧı

Republican party	республикалык	respublikalık
elections	шайлоо	ʃajloo
to elect (vt)	шайлоо	ʃajloo
elector, voter	шайлоочу	ʃajlootʃu
election campaign	шайлоо кампаниясы	ʃajloo kampanijası

voting (n)	добуш	dobuʃ
to vote (vi)	добуш берүү	dobuʃ beryy
suffrage, right to vote	добуш берүү укугу	dobuʃ beryy ukugu

candidate	талапкер	talapker
to be a candidate	талапкерлигин көрсөтүү	talapkerligin kørsøtyy
campaign	кампания	kampanija

| opposition (as adj) | оппозициялык | oppozitsijalık |
| opposition (n) | оппозиция | oppozitsija |

visit	визит	vizit
official visit	расмий визит	rasmij vizit
international (adj)	эл аралык	el aralık

| negotiations | сүйлөшүүлөр | syjløʃyylør |
| to negotiate (vi) | сүйлөшүүлөр жүргүзүү | syjløʃyylør dʒyrgyzyy |

193. Politics. Government. Part 2

society	коом	koom
constitution	конституция	konstitutsija
power (political control)	бийлик	bijlik
corruption	коррупция	korruptsija

| law (justice) | мыйзам | mıjzam |
| legal (legitimate) | мыйзамдуу | mıjzamduu |

| justice (fairness) | адилеттик | adilettik |
| just (fair) | адилеттүү | adilettyy |

committee	комитет	komitet
bill (draft law)	мыйзам долбоору	mıjzam dolbooru
budget	бюджет	bʉdʒet
policy	саясат	sajasat
reform	реформа	reforma
radical (adj)	радикалдуу	radikalduu

power (strength, force)	күч	kytʃ
powerful (adj)	кудуреттүү	kudurettyy
supporter	жактоочу	dʒaktootʃu
influence	таасир	taasir
regime (e.g., military ~)	түзүм	tyzym

conflict	чыр-чатак	tʃır-tʃatak
conspiracy (plot)	заговор	zagovor
provocation	айгак аракети	ajgak araketi
to overthrow (regime, etc.)	кулатуу	kulatuu
overthrow (of government)	кулатуу	kulatuu
revolution	ыңкылап	ıŋkılap
coup d'état	төңкөрүш	tøŋkøryʃ
military coup	аскердик төңкөрүш	askerdik tøŋkøryʃ
crisis	каатчылык	kaattʃılık
economic recession	экономикалык төмөндөө	ekonomikalık tømøndøø
demonstrator (protester)	демонстрант	demonstrant
demonstration	демонстрация	demonstratsija
martial law	согуш абалында	soguʃ abalında
military base	аскер базасы	asker bazası
stability	туруктуулук	turuktuuluk
stable (adj)	туруктуу	turuktuu
exploitation	эзүү	ezyy
to exploit (workers)	эзүү	ezyy
racism	расизм	rasizm
racist	расист	rasist
fascism	фашизм	faʃizm
fascist	фашист	faʃist

194. Countries. Miscellaneous

foreigner	чет өлкөлүк	tʃet ølkølyk
foreign (adj)	чет өлкөлүк	tʃet ølkølyk
abroad (in a foreign country)	чет өлкөдө	tʃet ølkødø
emigrant	эмигрант	emigrant
emigration	эмиграция	emigratsija
to emigrate (vi)	башка өлкөгө көчүү	baʃka ølkøgø køtʃyy
the West	Батыш	batıʃ
the East	Чыгыш	tʃıgıʃ
the Far East	Алыскы Чыгыш	alıskı tʃıgıʃ
civilization	цивилизация	tsıvilizatsija
humanity (mankind)	адамзат	adamzat
the world (earth)	аалам	aalam
peace	тынчтык	tıntʃtık
worldwide (adj)	дүйнөлүк	dyjnølyk

homeland	мекен	meken
people (population)	эл	el
population	калк	kalk
people (a lot of ~)	адамдар	adamdar
nation (people)	улут	ulut
generation	муун	muun

territory (area)	аймак	ajmak
region	регион	region
state (part of a country)	штат	ʃtat

tradition	салт	salt
custom (tradition)	үрп-адат	yrp-adat
ecology	экология	ekologija

Indian (Native American)	индеец	indeets
Gypsy (masc.)	цыган	tsıgan
Gypsy (fem.)	цыган аял	tsıgan ajal
Gypsy (adj)	цыгандык	tsıgandık

empire	империя	imperija
colony	колония	kolonija
slavery	кулчулук	kulʧuluk
invasion	басып келүү	basıp kelyy
famine	ачарчылык	atʃarʧılık

195. Major religious groups. Confessions

| religion | дин | din |
| religious (adj) | диний | dinij |

faith, belief	диний ишеним	dinij iʃenim
to believe (in God)	ишенүү	iʃenyy
believer	динчил	dinʧil

| atheism | атеизм | ateizm |
| atheist | атеист | ateist |

Christianity	Христианчылык	χristianʧılık
Christian (n)	христиан	χristian
Christian (adj)	христиандык	χristiandık

Catholicism	Католицизм	katolitsizm
Catholic (n)	католик	katolik
Catholic (adj)	католиктер	katolikter

Protestantism	Протестантизм	protestantizm
Protestant Church	Протестанттык чиркөө	protestanttık ʧirkøø
Protestant (n)	протестанттар	protestanttar
Orthodoxy	Православие	pravoslavie

Orthodox Church	Православдык чиркөө	pravoslavdık tʃirkøø
Orthodox (n)	православдык	pravoslavdık
Presbyterianism	Пресвитерианчылык	presviteriantʃılık
Presbyterian Church	Пресвитериандык чиркөө	presviteriandık tʃirkøø
Presbyterian (n)	пресвитериандык	presviteriandık
Lutheranism	Лютерандык чиркөө	lʉterandık tʃirkøø
Lutheran (n)	лютерандык	lʉterandık
Baptist Church	Баптизм	baptizm
Baptist (n)	баптист	baptist
Anglican Church	Англикан чиркөөсү	anglikan tʃirkøøsy
Anglican (n)	англикан	anglikan
Mormonism	Мормондук	mormonduk
Mormon (n)	мормон	mormon
Judaism	Иудаизм	iudaizm
Jew (n)	иудей	iudej
Buddhism	Буддизм	buddizm
Buddhist (n)	буддист	buddist
Hinduism	Индуизм	induizm
Hindu (n)	индуист	induist
Islam	Ислам	islam
Muslim (n)	мусулман	musulman
Muslim (adj)	мусулмандык	musulmandık
Shiah Islam	Шиизм	ʃiizm
Shiite (n)	шиит	ʃiit
Sunni Islam	Суннизм	sunnizm
Sunnite (n)	суннит	sunnit

196. Religions. Priests

priest	поп	pop
the Pope	Рим Папасы	rim papası
monk, friar	кечил	ketʃil
nun	кечил аял	ketʃil ajal
pastor	пастор	pastor
abbot	аббат	abbat
vicar (parish priest)	викарий	vikarij

| hishop | епископ | episkop |
| cardinal | кардинал | kardinal |

preacher	диний үгүттөөчү	dinij ygyttøøtʃy
preaching	үгүт	ygyt
parishioners	чиркөө коомунун мүчөлөрү	tʃirkøø koomunun mytʃøløry

| believer | динчил | dintʃil |
| atheist | атеист | ateist |

197. Faith. Christianity. Islam

| Adam | Адам ата | adam ata |
| Eve | Обо эне | obo ene |

God	Кудай	kudaj
the Lord	Алла талаа	alla talaa
the Almighty	Кудуреттүү	kudurettyy

sin	күнөө	kynøø
to sin (vi)	күнөө кылуу	kynøø kıluu
sinner (masc.)	күнөөкөр	kynøøkør
sinner (fem.)	күнөөкөр аял	kynøøkør ajal

| hell | тозок | tozok |
| paradise | бейиш | bejiʃ |

| Jesus | Иса | isa |
| Jesus Christ | Иса Пайгамбар | isa pajgambar |

the Holy Spirit	Ыйык Рух	ıjık ruχ
the Savior	Куткаруучу	kutkaruutʃu
the Virgin Mary	Бүбү Мариям	byby marijam

the Devil	Шайтан	ʃajtan
devil's (adj)	шайтан	ʃajtan
Satan	Шайтан	ʃajtan
satanic (adj)	шайтандык	ʃajtandık

angel	периште	periʃte
guardian angel	сактагыч периште	saktagıtʃ periʃte
angelic (adj)	периште	periʃte

apostle	апостол	apostol
archangel	архангель	arχangelʲ
the Antichrist	антихрист	antiχrist

| Church | Чиркөө | tʃirkøø |
| Bible | библия | biblija |

biblical (adj)	библиялык	biblijalık
Old Testament	Эзелки осуят	ezelki osujat
New Testament	Жаңы осуят	dʒaŋı osujat
Gospel	Евангелие	evangelie
Holy Scripture	Ыйык	ıjık
Heaven	Жаннат	dʒannat

Commandment	парз	parz
prophet	пайгамбар	pajgambar
prophecy	пайгамбар сөзү	pajgambar søzy

Allah	Аллах	allaχ
Mohammed	Мухаммед	muχammed
the Koran	Куран	kuran

mosque	мечит	metʃit
mullah	мулла	mulla
prayer	дуба	duba
to pray (vi, vt)	дуба кылуу	duba kıluu

pilgrimage	зыярат	zıjarat
pilgrim	зыяратчы	zıjarattʃı
Mecca	Мекке	mekke

church	чиркөө	tʃirkøø
temple	ибадаткана	ibadatkana
cathedral	чоң чиркөө	tʃoŋ tʃirkøø
Gothic (adj)	готикалуу	gotikaluu
synagogue	синагога	sinagoga
mosque	мечит	metʃit

chapel	кичинекей чиркөө	kitʃinekej tʃirkøø
abbey	аббаттык	abbattık
monastery	монастырь	monastırʲ

bell (church ~s)	коңгуроо	koŋguroo
bell tower	коңгуроо мунарасы	koŋguroo munarası
to ring (ab. bells)	коңгуроо кагуу	koŋguroo kaguu

cross	крест	krest
cupola (roof)	купол	kupol
icon	икона	ikona

soul	жан	dʒan
fate (destiny)	тагдыр	tagdır
evil (n)	жамандык	dʒamandık
good (n)	жакшылык	dʒakʃılık

vampire	кан соргуч	kan sorgutʃ
witch (evil ~)	жез тумшук	dʒez tumʃuk
demon	шайтан	ʃajtan
spirit	арбак	arbak

redemption (giving us ~)	күнөөнү жуу	kynøøny dʒuu
to redeem (vt)	күнөөнү жуу	kynøøny dʒuu
church service, mass	ибадат	ibadat
to say mass	ибадат кылуу	ibadat kıluu
confession	сыр төгүү	sır tøgyy
to confess (vi)	сыр төгүү	sır tøgyy
saint (n)	ыйык	ıjık
sacred (holy)	ыйык	ıjık
holy water	ыйык суу	ıjık suu
ritual (n)	диний ырым-жырым	dinij ırım-dʒırım
ritual (adj)	диний ырым-жырым	dinij ırım-dʒırım
sacrifice	курмандык	kurmandık
superstition	ырым-жырым	ırım-dʒırım
superstitious (adj)	ырымчыл	ırımtʃıl
afterlife	тиги дүйнө	tigi dyjnø
eternal life	түбөлүк жашоо	tybølyk dʒaʃoo

MISCELLANEOUS

198. Various useful words

background (green ~)	фон	fon
balance (of situation)	теңдем	teŋdem
barrier (obstacle)	тоскоолдук	toskoolduk
base (basis)	түп	typ
beginning	башталыш	baʃtalıʃ
category	категория	kategorija
cause (reason)	себеп	sebep
choice	тандоо	tandoo
coincidence	дал келгендик	dal kelgendik
comfortable (~ chair)	ыңгайлуу	ıŋgajluu
comparison	салыштырма	salıʃtırma
compensation	ордун толтуруу	ordun tolturuu
degree (extent, amount)	даража	daradʒa
development	өнүгүү	ønygyy
difference	айырма	ajırma
effect (e.g., of drugs)	таасир	taasir
effort (exertion)	күч аракет	kyʧ araket
element	элемент	element
end (finish)	бүтүү	bytyy
example (illustration)	мисал	misal
fact	далил	dalil
frequent (adj)	бат-бат	bat-bat
growth (development)	өсүү	øsyy
help	жардам	dʒardam
ideal	идеал	ideal
kind (sort, type)	түр	tyr
labyrinth	лабиринт	labirint
mistake, error	ката	kata
moment	учур	uʧur
object (thing)	объект	obʰjekt
obstacle	тоскоолдук	toskoolduk
original (original copy)	түпнуска	typnuska
part (~ of sth)	бөлүгү	bølygy
particle, small part	бөлүкчө	bølykʧø
pause (break)	тыныгуу	tınıguu

position	позиция	pozitsija
principle	усул	usul
problem	көйгөй	køjgøj

process	жараян	dʒarajan
progress	өнүгүү	ønygyy
property (quality)	касиет	kasiet
reaction	реакция	reaktsija
risk	тобокел	tobokel

secret	сыр	sɯr
series	катар	katar
shape (outer form)	тариз	tariz
situation	кырдаал	kɯrdaal
solution	чечүү	tʃetʃyy

standard (adj)	стандарттуу	standarttuu
standard (level of quality)	стандарт	standart
stop (pause)	токтотуу	toktotuu
style	стиль	stilʲ

system	тутум	tutum
table (chart)	жадыбал	dʒadɯbal
tempo, rate	темп	temp
term (word, expression)	атоо	atoo

thing (object, item)	буюм	bujɯm
truth (e.g., moment of ~)	чындык	tʃɯndɯk
turn (please wait your ~)	кезек	kezek
type (sort, kind)	түр	tyr
urgent (adj)	шашылыш	ʃaʃɯlɯʃ

urgently (adv)	шашылыш	ʃaʃɯlɯʃ
utility (usefulness)	пайда	pajda
variant (alternative)	вариант	variant
way (means, method)	ыкма	ɯkma
zone	алкак	alkak